Wembley End of an Era

contents.   5 Introduction.   6 The Start of Wembley Stadium.   7 A Legend in the Making.   8 The Empire

Exhibition.   9 Arthur Elvin.   10 The New Stadium.   12 Thanks for the Memories.   28 Cup Final.   32 STOP PRESS

Cup Final 2000.   34 Roll of Honour.   36 The Magnificent Seven.   50 The Giantkillers.   55 So Near and Yet

So Far.   62 Over the Moon/Sick as a Parrot.   64 The World Comes to Wembley.   66 The Agony and the Ecstasy.

68 World Cup at Wembley.   72 Euro 96.   76 The Tartan Army.   78 European Champions Cup Final.

80 European Cup-Winners Cup.   82 Rugby at Wembley.   86 Wonderful Wigan.   88 The Olympic Games.

90 Boxing at Wembley.   92 Other Sports at Wembley.   94 Music at Wembley.   96 The Final Whistle.

A Letter from Mark Wood

This End of an Era book truly captures the most significant and poignant moments in the history of football and The FA Cup at Wembley.

The FA Cup competition has reached millions of people all over the world ever since Wembley's history began with Bolton Wanderers lifting the Cup in 1923.

Few have not been touched by the magic of The FA Cup Final at Wembley, from the walk up Wembley Way, through the twin towers onto the hallowed turf and finally the long climb up the famous 39 steps.

As the sponsor of The FA Cup, AXA is proud to be involved in the End of an Era and will be hosting the last ever event on the pitch at Wembley which promises to be a very special and emotional occasion.

During Wembley's demolition and re-birth, AXA will continue to support football and The FA Cup. We will continue to operate the Kits in the Community scheme, launched by Michael Owen and Jamie Redknapp, which provides schools and clubs with football strips. The FA Cup Roadshow will take the Cup around the country giving supporters a chance to lift the most famous domestic trophy in the world.

We also support women's football, and will continue to assist The Football Association in further raising the profile of the UK's fastest growing sport.

As Wembley approaches the end of a magnificent 77 years you can rest assured that AXA's sponsorship of The FA Cup will extend the magic to many more real life supporters.

Yours

Mark Wood
Group Chief Executive
AXA

introduction

Wembley Stadium is known all over the world as the greatest stage, the venue of legends and the place where every boy who can kick a ball dreams of playing. Now, as it closes its doors for the last time to make way for a 21st century superstadium, its place in history is assured. We celebrate its illustrious past in these pages – and present a selection of its great moments.

If Wembley Stadium is the place, then Football is the game and the FA Cup Final is the event. To appear in a Cup Final at Wembley, win or lose, is the pinnacle of any player's career. We look at the great clubs that have dominated the Cup Final and the giantkillers who had one moment of glory. Find out where your team stands on the Wembley Roll of Honour.

Wembley Stadium has also witnessed the agony and the ecstasy of England's international football history, from the devastating defeat by the Hungarians in 1953 to its greatest moment of triumph at the 1966 World Cup. But Wembley has been more than a national football stadium: the most prestigious event of the Rugby League calendar, the Challenge Cup Final, is played there, it has hosted the 1948 Olympic Games and staged the most memorable match in British boxing, Cassius Clay v Henry Cooper. Nor is its glory confined to sport. Who could forget Live Aid and all the other major rock music events of recent years? Whether you are a sportsman or a rock star, to appear at Wembley is the fulfilment of a dream.

Nowhere on the planet has seen such a concentration of emotion and adrenaline. As the bulldozers go in, they may destroy a structure of bricks and mortar, but the spirit of Wembley Stadium is indestructible and will take its tradition to the new stadium. Until then you have this book to remind you!

Wembley Stadium

Although this book celebrates the years from 1923, the site of the stadium has been associated with sport and entertainment for well over 100 years.

In Victorian days in a leafy outer London suburb, there was a lovely park with fountains and flowerbeds, waterfalls and walkways. There were also football and cricket pitches and a running track. Wembley Park Leisure Grounds was very much a local amenity until 1889 when the Metropolitan Railway decided that a major attraction, linked to central London by railway line, would encourage more people to use their trains.

No doubt inspired by the recently completed Eiffel Tower, they began to build a four-legged steel tower 1,150 ft (350m) high in Wembley Park, conveniently close to the railway line. The ambitious plans included a nightclub and turkish baths halfway up, making the Millennium Dome sound like a tea party in a scout hut in comparison.

Sadly, the tower only reached 200ft (61m) before the scheme ran out of money and was abandoned. Watkin's Folly (named after the chairman of the Metropolitan Railway) became a tourist attraction in its own right for many years, before being blown up in 1907. It would have been amazing

to have had a tower even bigger than the Eiffel Tower (only 1,051ft, 320m) in London. This would have been the tallest building in the world until the Empire State Building surpassed it in 1931. However, if the project had succeeded Wembley Stadium would never have existed, because Watkin's Tower was on the very same site.

Years passed but the sporting link remained - Wembley Park had become a golf course. After the First World War, the Government hoped to boost morale with a British Empire Exhibition and chose Wembley Park as the site, despite the seven mile distance from central London. The money was raised, with some difficulty for these were lean times, by public subscription.

Significantly and crucially for the commercial viability of the scheme, The Football Association gave £10,000 towards the million plus total. They made a deal with The British Exhibition (1924) Inc., a privately owned corporation, which gave The FA the right to hold Final Ties "and other such matches as may be agreed", for 21 years. The die was cast.

Sir Robert McAlpine took time off from overseeing the building work to write *The Story of the Building of the Greatest Stadium in the World* (1923). True to the then-prevailing spirit of nationalism and imperialism, he wrote: "When Titus of Ancient Rome built the vast Amphitheatre, known on account of its colossal size as the Colosseum, taking 16 years to do the job, it probably did not enter his imperial mind that one day a Stadium almost three times as large, and infinitely more enduring, would be constructed in less than a tenth of the time by a nation whose people he and his forbears thought it scarcely worthwhile to conquer."

a legend in the making

Bigger than the Roman Colosseum, higher than the walls of Jericho, the old Wembley Stadium was famous before it was even built.

The Empire Stadium, as it was first known, was designed and built as the focal point of the Empire Exhibition of 1924. Essentially a trade and morale boosting exercise, the exhibition would also feature sport and entertainment and provide jobs for many of the thousands of men who returned home from the trenches to find mass unemployment.

Building the stadium was the first job to be done. The first turf was cut by the Duke of York (the future King George VI) on January 10th 1922. Sir Robert McAlpine & Sons were the building contractors. The site was levelled - there had been a hill, so 150,000 tons of clay had to be taken away. 25,000 tons of ferro-concrete were needed to make the foundations and the outside walls, 900 tons of steel girders supported the stands and terraces and half a million rivets held the whole thing together. It had 37 concrete arches each with a 50ft span and - most famously - a pair of domed concrete towers, 126 ft high, either side of the entrance. At 890 ft (271m) long by 650 ft (198m) wide, it was boasted that the new stadium would be bigger than the Colosseum in Rome.

The resulting building was the work of architects Sir John Simpson and Maxwell Ayrton, and engineer Owen Williams.

Narrow gauge trains were used to bring materials into the site: to get the last one out would have meant dismantling something already built so the train was buried, according to legend, under the arena. The stadium took 300 days of frenzied activity to build. They had a deadline set by their first paying customer, The Football Association. The first Cup Final at Wembley took place just three days after the stadium was finished in April 1923. As a safety test 1,200 soldiers were brought in to sit, stand and stamp their feet on the stands and terraces. Luckily the building survived.

In the fund raising appeal speech given by the Prince of Wales, the stadium was envisaged as a national sportsground. The Football Association was seeking a permanent home for The FA Cup Final and put £10,000 into the appeal fund (previous Cup Finals had recently been held at The Oval, Crystal Palace and Stamford Bridge). The City of Glasgow generously gave £100,000. The final bill came to £750,000.

the empire exhibition

Originally called the Empire Stadium, Wembley Stadium was built as the centrepiece of the 1924 Empire Exhibition.

above: East meets west at the exotic Hong Kong building. below: King George and Queen Mary take the King and Queen of Romania to see the sights.

Although it did not actually take place until a year after the first Cup Final was held at Wembley, the stadium would not have been built without the great exhibition. Such an undertaking could never have got off the ground without government backing. Even so it made a spectacular loss; total costs for the exhibition were put at £12 million, some £10 million more than anticipated. However, some 27 million paying customers agreed it was the greatest show on earth and you can't argue with that.

The exhibition was opened on St George's Day, April 23rd 1924, by King George V and Queen Mary. His opening speech was his first ever broadcast to the nation. There was a colourful royal procession around the stadium, the king and queen riding in the state carriage.

The stadium was the largest building and the scene of many spectaculars: an Empire Pageant, an International Rodeo (400 cattle plus 400 horses), a Boy Scout Jamboree, an Imperial Choir so big that the choir itself filled half the stadium, a Military Tattoo, circuses and firework displays. One of the more bizarre events was a show called London Defended, which featured small planes, illuminated with fairy lights attached to them, flying over the stadium and dropping incendiary bombs. The resulting fires were then quickly and reassuringly put out by firemen, to the cheers of the audience.

Sport played a part even in these early days. A rugby union match between the Army and the RAF took place, as did two Cup Finals (1924 and 1925), which were considered part of the exhibition. There was also a boxing match between light-heavyweight Jack Bloomfield and the American Tom Gibbons.

The stadium was one of four gigantic buildings housing the exhibition: there were Palaces of Industry, Engineering and Art, and hundreds of pavilions in the architectural style of the countries exhibiting inside them. These buildings were set inside 219 acres of theme-park attractions; a boating lake, a roller coaster, a water chute and a scenic railway running continually around the park. One wonders if a young Walt Disney was one of the 90,000 people an hour who visited the exhibition at its peak. Certainly there has never been anything like it since in the United Kingdom (Alton Towers notwithstanding).

After less than two years, the exhibition was closed in October 1925. It was reckoned that everybody who wanted to had seen it by now. The idea of a permanent attraction, with continual improvements and aggressive advertising a la Disney was light years ahead. Perhaps because it had been a financial disaster, the buildings were hurriedly sold off or demolished: the exotic East African pavilion became a jam factory, for example. What a waste!

above left: The Indian pavilion in front of the Canadian building. **centre:** The Duke and Duchess of York attend the opening ceremony. **above right:** The Royal Procession does the first Wembley lap of honour.

Arthur Elvin

The man who made Wembley Stadium what it is started his thirty year career there running a tobacco kiosk.

When the government pulled the plug on the Empire Exhibition in the autumn of 1925, the operating company went into liquidation within weeks. What would become of the site, now desolate and described as "a vast white elephant, a rotting sepulchre of hopes and the grave of fortunes" ?

It was put up for auction but failed to make the reserve price (£350,000). Nobody wanted it. Eventually the price was dropped to £300,000 and it was snapped up by speculator Jimmy White. White paid a 10 per cent deposit and gave the job of dismantling the buildings, which he intended to sell off at a profit, to Arthur Elvin.

Elvin was a young man of respectable but humble origins, who had been in the RAF during the First World War. His plane had been forced down and he had been taken prisoner of war. After the Armistice, he was employed in dismantling ammunition dumps in France and this is where he learned about demolition. Those promoting the idea of the Empire Exhibition had laid heavy emphasis on the employment potential of the proj-

ect. Elvin was one of the many penniless, ex-servicemen who came looking for a job and he got one in a tobacco kiosk for £4.10s a week. By the time the exhibition closed, Elvin owned eight kiosks and had expanded into confectionery and souvenirs. Elvin saw how money could be made selling off buildings and made a good profit on the deal. As fast as the buildings were taken down, they were packed off on a lorry and rebuilt elsewhere.

Elvin could see the potential in the stadium itself. He had seen first hand how hungry the British public were for entertainment and events on a grand scale. In 1927 he offered White £122,500 for the site. He paid £12,500 as a deposit on a ten year mortgage, however White, who was faced with bankruptcy, committed suicide a few months later. This left Elvin in a terrible position. Instead of ten years to come up with the remaining £110,000, the Official Receiver gave him two weeks to pay the balance or lose his deposit. Elvin now showed his true entrepreneurial colours: he put together a syndicate which agreed to buy the stadium for £150,000. At 6.30pm on August 17th 1927 he bought the stadium from the Official Receiver for £110,000; one minute later he sold it to the Wembley Stadium and Greyhound Racecourse Company

(managing director Arthur Elvin) for £150,000. He took his profit in shares and thus became the boss at Wembley.

For the next thirty years or so he dominated proceedings at Wembley, making the stadium a going concern and a national institution. In 1946 his contribution towards British sport was recognised with a knighthood. In 1957 Sir Arthur died suddenly while on a cruise. He takes a special place in the Wembley Hall of Fame.

Though no stadium can ever top Wembley for atmosphere and historical association, there are now bigger and better equipped stadiums in the world. Technological advances, safety requirements and rising expectations of comfort for both players and the public have called into question Wembley Stadium's future. Not all the spectators had an equally good view of the football: the grey-hound/athletics track kept the audience from the field and roof supports obstructed the view. In 1923 people didn't mind getting a good soaking during a match; now if it rains - and it often does - the gate money would go down if there wasn't a roof over the spectators. Players and performers nowadays expect a level of luxury in the dressing rooms and bathrooms: many of them are millionaires after all. Despite several modernisations there is no room to expand. Ironically

the measure taken to preserve the building (making it a listed building, which means it cannot alter its external appearance or expand beyond its walls) means that to make room for change it will have to be demolished.

A plan for a new national stadium was hatched between the Sports' Council and the governing bodies of football, rugby league and athletics. There was no doubt about the need for such a stadium and there was National Lottery money available to help finance it. The only question was: where would it be? Bradford, Sheffield and Birmingham wanted it, but eventually the choice was narrowed to Manchester or Wembley. Manchester had twice bid for the Olympics and had a site ready, but their Millennium Stadium failed to win, partly because of its poor public transport facilities. Wembley's capital city location, with rail, underground

new stadium

The National Stadium, capable of hosting the world's greatest sporting events, will be open for business - subject to planning permission - in 2003. World-class comfort, the highest safety standards and perfect sight lines will ensure that Wembley retains its legendary status.

and road access all excellent was the trump card and who could take seriously a World Cup or Olympic bid that didn't revolve around Wembley?

The key view of Wembley Stadium for most visiting fans is the walk up Olympic Way towards the main facade and towers. The designers have been at pains to replicate this experience in the new stadium. This is why so much importance has been attached to the fate of the twin towers. At first it was hoped that the towers would remain and somehow be incorporated into the new building. However, for sound, but complex, engineering reasons, the towers have to go. They are replaced with a spectacular 133m high arch. This will tower over the 52m stadium and provide a dramatic landmark across the city. The arch provides exciting opportunities for spectacular lighting effects at night.

The front facade follows the model of the original with a Banqueting Hall sitting between two 'bookends'. The design team refers to this as the Wembley smile. Circulation spaces run off the side of this. In the new stadium circulation will be by escalator rather than staircase.

Maintaining the quality of Wembley's world famous pitch, while designing a new stadium that is considerably taller than the existing building, and placing fans closer to the pitch, has been a major challenge for the design team. Using computer models of air movement and sunlight on the existing pitch, a unique moving roof has been designed for the new stadium. This will be left open between events but can be moved to line up with the touchline within 15 minutes, ensuring every spectator is sheltered during an event. In bright sunlight the roof can be withdrawn to allow clear TV pictures. At 3pm on Cup Final Day, for instance, only the two southern corner flags will be in shadow.

The acoustics of the new ground take the current ground as a benchmark. Recordings made during the 1999 FA Cup Final and models of the stadium created by using three blasts of white noise during England v Poland earlier that year form the basis of sophisticated computer models that allowed the design team to tune the acoustics of the new stadium.

The new stadium seats 90,000. This is 10,000 more than at present. The individual seats are more generous. Disabled supporters will find their needs well provided for with 400 wheelchair spaces.

Football and rugby spectators will be closer to the action. The front row of each stand is closer to the pitch with the front row at each end being between 9m and 13m from the touchline (compared with up to 40m in the old stadium). This allows the distance to the centre spot from each end to remain 136m despite adding 10,000 seats to the capacity of the ground. The spectators in the back row have considerably better views than before. The seating in the new stadium is more steeply raked and there are no obstructed views.

The old stadium was built in an age of low expectation of public food, with many of the service points unable to serve chilled drinks. The new stadium has 478 food service points (up from 152) able to offer modern standards of catering. Well-known brands will be providing food at high street prices and cold beer and other drinks at pub prices. Toilet provision has increased 5.5fold. There are also 13 restaurants including a Banqueting Hall seating 2000, 100,000 sq ft of office space, and a museum of Wembley history.

To update visit: www.wembleynationalstadium.com

left: **A vision of the future: the English National Stadium.**
right: **Architects Lord Foster and Rod Sheard unveil the exciting new design at a press conference in 1999.**

thanks for the memories

As Wembley Stadium moves into the pages of history, interest in Wembley memorabilia is mounting. The programmes, badges, medals etc that were issued for each unique occasion have a value that goes beyond mere money. They are the tangible proof that the occasion took place and the person who first owned them was actually there. They provide an instant memory trigger and a welcome chance to wallow in nostalgia. In the next few pages we display some of the treasured items that memories are made of.

the first cup final

Saturday April 28th 1923

The very first Wembley Cup Final, now known as the
White Horse Final, attracted about 250,000 spectators.
In terms of crowd control and good humour it was a
triumph snatched from the jaws of disaster, and it
made a spectacular debut for the new stadium.

above: **The first Wembley Cup Final souvenir programme and a ticket. Many
enjoyed the match without benefit of either.**

SUNDAY PICTORIAL, April 29, 1923.

FINAL WEEKS OF £7,000 FILM CONTEST — See Page 5

SUNDAY · PICTORIAL

SALE MORE THAN DOUBLE THAT OF ANY OTHER SUNDAY PICTURE PAPER

No. 424. | Registered at the G.P.O. as a Newspaper. | SUNDAY, APRIL 29, 1923 | [24 PAGES] | Twopence.

WEMBLEY STADIUM STORMED BY EXCITED CUP FINAL CROWDS

A striking aerial photograph of the scene at Wembley Stadium yesterday after the gates had been closed. All accommodation is packed, spectators flood the playing pitch, while thousands clustered outside are clamouring for admittance.

One of four daring souls who climbed a drain-pipe to secure an entrance at the back of the lofty covered stand.

Police holding back would-be spectators at the entrance to the tunnel leading to the pitch.

Police arriving by motor-van at the ground in response to a call for reinforcements.

The crowd swarming over the closed turnstiles the instruction to "Pay Here."

The most amazing Cup final on record was won by Bolton Wanderers yesterday, when they defeated West Ham United by two clear goals at the Empire Stadium, Wembley. The start was delayed for three-quarters of an hour by the most extraordinary scenes. The gates were closed with thousands still waiting for admission, though the spectators within had broken through to the running track around the ground and invaded the play itself. The crowd outside rushed the ground, clambering over the turnstiles, and confusion even greater. With the arrival of the King, mounted police managed pitch just clear. Pictures of play on page 24.

above: Cup winner's medal, front and back, awarded to R. Haworth of Bolton. **left:** The next day's paper makes no mention of the famous white horse. **below:** David Jack, first man to score a goal at Wembley.

FOOTBALL ASSOC.
STEWARD
FINAL TIE 1923

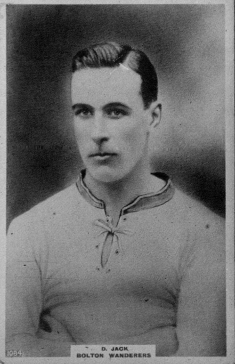

D. JACK
BOLTON WANDERERS

above: The official badge worn by one of the stewards.

Wembley Cup Fina...

From a hand-printed sheet in the 1920s to the lavish souvenir programmes of today.

1923   1924   1925   1926   1927

1933   1934   1935   1936   1937

1948   1949   1950   1951   1952

programmes

1928

1929

1930

1931

1932

1938

1939

1946

1947

1953

1954

1955

1956

1957 **1958** **1959** **1960** **1961**

1966 **1967** **1968** **1969**

1973 **1974** **1975** **1976**

1981 **1981** REPLAY **1982** **1982** REPLAY

THE FOOTBALL ASSOCIATION CHALLENGE CUP COMPETITION

FINAL TIE
BURNLEY
v
TOTTENHAM HOTSPUR
(Holders)
SATURDAY, MAY 5th, 1962. KICK-OFF 3 p.m.

EMPIRE STADIUM
WEMBLEY

OFFICIAL PROGRAMME   ONE SHILLING

1962

THE FOOTBALL ASSOCIATION CHALLENGE CUP COMPETITION

THE FOOTBALL ASSOCIATION CENTENARY YEAR

FINAL TIE
LEICESTER CITY
v
MANCHESTER UNITED

OFFICIAL PROGRAMME   ONE SHILLING

WEMBLEY
EMPIRE STADIUM

SATURDAY, MAY 25th, Kick-off 3 pm

1963

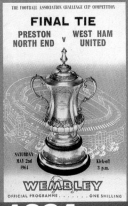

THE FOOTBALL ASSOCIATION CHALLENGE CUP COMPETITION

FINAL TIE
PRESTON NORTH END v WEST HAM UNITED

SATURDAY MAY 2nd 1964   Kick-off 3 p.m.

WEMBLEY

OFFICIAL PROGRAMME . . . . . . ONE SHILLING

1964

EMPIRE STADIUM

THE FOOTBALL ASSOCIATION CHALLENGE CUP COMPETITION

FINAL TIE

WEMBLEY

LEEDS UNITED
VERSUS
LIVERPOOL

Official Programme   One Shilling

SATURDAY MAY 1st 1965, Kick-off 3p.m.

1965

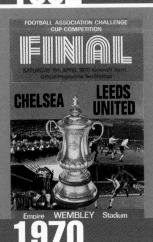

FOOTBALL ASSOCIATION CHALLENGE CUP COMPETITION

FINAL
SATURDAY 11th APRIL 1970 Kick-off 3 p.m.
Official Programme Two Shillings

CHELSEA
v
LEEDS UNITED

Empire   WEMBLEY   Stadium

1970

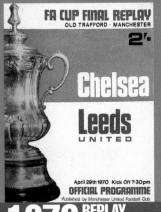

FA CUP FINAL REPLAY
OLD TRAFFORD · MANCHESTER

2'-

Chelsea
v
Leeds
UNITED

April 29th 1970 Kick Off 7·30pm
OFFICIAL PROGRAMME
Published by Manchester United Football Club

1970 REPLAY OLD TRAFFORD

ARSENAL v LIVERPOOL
FOOTBALL ASSOCIATION CHALLENGE CUP COMPETITION

FINAL
SATURDAY 8th MAY 1971
Kick off 3 pm
Official Programme . . . 10p

1971

FOOTBALL ASSOCIATION CHALLENGE CUP COMPETITION

1872   CENTENARY YEAR   1972

FINAL
SATURDAY 6th MAY 1972 . . . . . KICK-OFF 3 pm.

ARSENAL v LEEDS UNITED

EMPIRE **WEMBLEY** STADIUM
Official Souvenir Programme 15p

1972

FOOTBALL ASSOCIATION CHALLENGE CUP COMPETITION

FINAL

Liverpool
v
Manchester United

SATURDAY 21st MAY 1977 Kick off 3pm

WEMBLEY STADIUM
Silver Jubilee Year Official Cup Final Programme 50p

1977

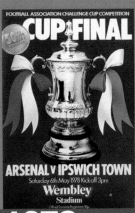

CUP FINAL

ARSENAL V IPSWICH TOWN
Saturday 6th May 1978 Kick off 3pm
Wembley
Stadium
Official Souvenir Programme 50p

1978

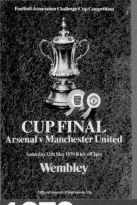

Football Association Challenge Cup Competition

CUP FINAL
Arsenal v Manchester United
Saturday 12th May 1979 Kick off 3pm
Wembley
Official Souvenir Programme 50p

1979

FOOTBALL ASSOCIATION CHALLENGE CUP COMPETITION

FINAL
ARSENAL v WEST HAM UNITED

Saturday
10th May 1980
Kick off 3pm
Wembley
Stadium
OFFICIAL SOUVENIR PROGRAMME 80p

1980

FOOTBALL ASSOCIATION CHALLENGE CUP COMPETITION

BRIGHTON & HOVE ALBION

CUP FINAL
Saturday 21st May 1983 Kick off 3pm

v

MANCHESTER UNITED

Wembley Stadium
Official Souvenir Programme 60p

1983

FOOTBALL ASSOCIATION CHALLENGE CUP FINAL

REPLAY

Thursday 26th May 1983 Kick Off 7.00pm

Brighton & Hove Albion
v

Wembley Stadium
Official Souvenir Programme 60p

1983 REPLAY

FOOTBALL ASSOCIATION CHALLENGE CUP COMPETITION

CUP FINAL

SATURDAY 19 MAY 1984
KICK-OFF 3.00p.m.

EVERTON
v
WATFORD

Wembley
Stadium

1984

FOOTBALL ASSOCIATION CHALLENGE CUP COMPETITION

CUP FINAL
·1985·

EVERTON   MANCHESTER UTD.
v

Wembley
OFFICIAL SOUVENIR PROGRAMME £1.00
SATURDAY 18th MAY 1985 KICKOFF 3PM

1985

1986

1987

1988

1989

1990

1990 REPLAY

1991

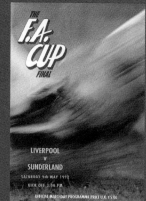

1992

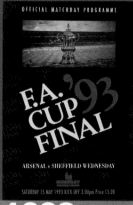

1993

1993 REPLAY

1994

1995

1996

1997

1998

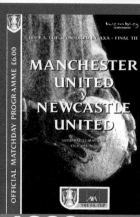

1999

medals and steward's badges

1939-40 war time cup winner's medal. West Ham beat Blackburn 1-0. Medals are normally made of gold, but as the war dragged on it was decided not to waste gold on medals.

A selection of steward's badges mostly from Wembley's early years when the designs were more varied. The badges are made of enamel and non-precious metal.

1932-33 runners up medal awarded to W. Dale of Manchester City, who lost to Everton.

1947-48 runners up medal awarded to A. Munro of Blackpool, who lost to Manchester United.

1974-75 cup winner's medal awarded to Tommy Taylor of West Ham, who beat Fulham.

above: Boots from the 1950s and the England v Netherlands cap (1969-70). above right: Scotland shirt from the 1950s. centre: Arsenal shirt worn by Pat Rice at the 1971 Final.

kit & equipment

top: Allan Clarke's shirt from the 1972 Leeds win over Arsenal. It is signed inside the collar. above: The pre-war England shirt badge.

below: 1979 Arsenal v Manchester United. right: 1976 Manchester United v Southampton.

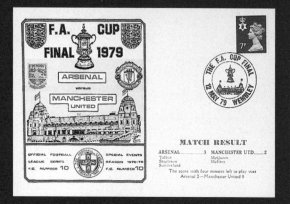

Cup Final postal covers

Postal covers were issued from the 1970s to commemorate Cup Finals. They were postmarked with the special Wembley hand stamp. A choice of design was available on each occasion.

Plate commemorating Sunderland's win over Leeds United in 1973. It is signed by the team.

Plate commemorating Southampton's 1976 victory over Manchester United. Signed by the players.

Plate commemorating Coventry City's triumph over Tottenham Hotspur in 1987. Signed by the team.

commemorative plates

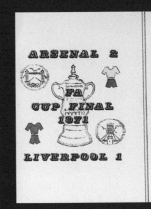

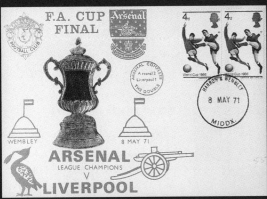

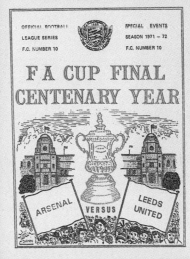

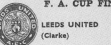

right, clockwise from top left: 1975 West Ham v Fulham, 1971 Arsenal v Liverpool, 1972 Arsenal v Leeds United, 1971 Arsenal v Liverpool.

WEMBLEY STADIUM

SPECIAL CAR PARK

WEMBLEY STADIUM

SPECIAL CAR PARK

WEMBLEY STADIUM

SPECIAL CAR PARK

1966

WATNEY MANN
WORLD CUP
SPECIAL PALE ALE
1966

left: Commemorative pennant produced by
Watney Mann, who were licensed to use the
World Cup Willie logo. From the sublime - a
ticket to the Final (above) - to the ridiculous - a
souvenir tea towel (right).

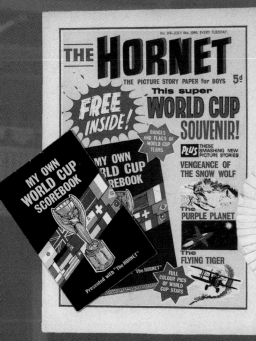

from left to right: **England shirt, tie, winner's medal, car park stickers, postcard signed by the ref, special issue of the boys' comic *The Hornet* with a free scorebook, rosette, cine films of the Final.**

World Cup

from left to right: **The official souvenir programme for the tournament, a programme for the Final, commemorative glass and beer bottle. Watney Mann brewed a special beer for the World Cup.**

below: A football ice bucket, perfect to chill the celebration champagne; a commemorative headscarf or a choice of tea towels to placate the missus, and a replica trophy for the serious football fantasist.

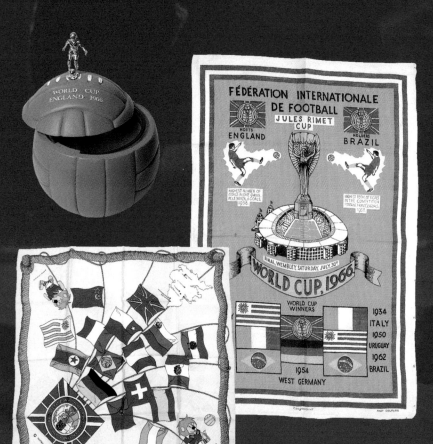

left: There was no escaping World Cup Willie, the official mascot of England's World Cup Squad. The 1966 World Cup was the first seriously commercialised tournament and as a result an astonishing variety of souvenirs and commemorative items were available. Regardless of taste and original value all the 1966 World Cup memorabilia is highly collectable.

pensions | life assurance | investments | insurance

The best competition in the world.

Nothing compares to playing in The F.A. Cup, which is why the competition continues to attract the world's best players. It has a unique history stretching back to 1871, when 15 teams took part and 2000 fans watched the first F.A. Cup Final at the Kennington Oval. This year's final, sponsored by AXA, has attracted 580 entries, and 80,000 fans will watch the final at

Wembley along with a global TV audience of over 400 million. AXA are proud sponsors of what is still surely the best club competition in the world. Their continued support also covers Youth Training programmes, The AXA Women's F.A. Cup, The AXA Women's Premier League, The AXA Women's Premier League Cup and of course your local teams.

REAL LIFE SUPPORTERS

www.axa.co.uk

All the events that take place at Wembley Stadium are special

CUP FINAL

but one annual event more than any other is associated in the public's mind with Wembley –

The Football Association Cup Final. 77 years of Wembley Cup Finals have seen their fair

share of drama, heartbreak and humour.

Cup Champions Manchester United have won the Cup 9 times at Wembley, making them the champion of champions. Arsenal come second with 7 wins and Spurs are third with 6. Arsenal, however, have made regular appearances at Wembley Cup Finals from the start whereas Manchester United's dominance is post Second World War.

Always the Bridesmaid? Liverpool and Arsenal both reached the final only to lose 5 times. Everton, Manchester United and Leicester City fell at the final post 4 times. Pity poor Leicester who have never won at Wembley.

The White Horse Final The first Cup Final at Wembley on April 28 1923 could easily have been the last. It is estimated that 250,000 people squeezed into a stadium designed for 120,000. No-one thought of selling a set number of tickets in advance and crowd control was non-existent. The situation was saved by one policeman on a white horse. Constable Scorey and Billy persuaded the spectators to step back off the pitch and eventually the game was started 46 minutes late. Players fell into the crowd on the touchline, spectators almost certainly kicked the ball more

than once and a goal was nearly disallowed when the ball sprang back out of the net due to the crush of people standing behind the goal. The occasion was seen at the time as a great success, a tribute to the good humour of all.

A Golden Oldie Sadly the late Bobby Moore played his last Wembley Final for 2nd Division Fulham in 1975 only to be beaten by his former club West Ham. Moore was philosophic about it to team-mate Alan Mullery. "At our age we shouldn't be playing in a Cup Final. Enjoy it while you can," said the sprightly 34-year-old.

Broken Bones No substitutes were allowed in a Cup Final until 1967. Despite the obvious fact that no sane player would fake an injury and leave the pitch in a Cup Final, the powers that be resisted pressure from players

above left: The *Graf Zeppelin* passing over Wembley Stadium during the 1930 Cup Final between Arsenal and Huddersfield.

left: The save that broke Bert Trautmann's neck in the 1956 Cup Final.

and fans alike for years because they feared they would open the flood gates for all kinds of play-acting. As if!

Meanwhile let us remember the heroic Manchester City goalie Bert Trautmann who broke his neck with 15 minutes to go, yet played on to the end rather than leave his team-mates with an unguarded goal.

In 1959 Roy Dwight scored a goal for Nottingham Forest then broke his leg in a tackle. He was carried off but the ten remaining managed to win. In 1984 Dwight's nephew, Reg, made a striking debut at Wembley as Elton John. By remaining on a piano stool he kept his limbs intact.

Can You Hear Me, Mother?
The 1928 final between Blackburn Rovers and Huddersfield Town was the first final to be broadcast on BBC Radio. George Allison was the commentator and he described the match from his box in the midst of the crowd, without the assistance of cameras but with helpful comments from nearby spectators.

To cope with the pressure of describing a fast moving match to 10 million listeners, he imagined that he was explaining it all to his elderly mother - a keen football fan. Listeners were aided by a black and white photograph published in the *Radio Times*, which showed a plan of the pitch divided into eight sections. His commentary was the first occasion when the phrase "back to square one" was heard.

Allison was able to tell his audience which players had the ball and which part of the pitch they were on. Unspoilt by colour television, action replays and a panel of celebrity commentators, the 1928 football fan was thrilled to be present at the match whilst remaining in his armchair, plan on his knees, wireless close by, all through the wonders of modern technology.

Sky Sport
In 1930 the Huddersfield-Arsenal game was literally overshadowed by the sinister presence of an illegally low-flying German airship, the *Graf Zeppelin*. Presumably its wealthy passengers wanted a bird's eye view of the match and it hovered directly over the pitch for several minutes.

Aerial activity returned in 1937 when a dispute over newsreel filming rights led to rival companies buzzing the ground in small planes and 'auto-gyros', as they called these primitive helicopters, during the match.

Lucky for Some
The 1970s was the decade of the underdog when a number of lower ranking clubs challenged the big stars. In 1973 Second Division Sunderland beat Leeds United, a team of International players, 1-0. Sunderland goalie, Jim Montgomery, was Man of the Match with a string of amazing saves. Later he exclaimed incredulously "When I die I shall have my left hand embalmed."

Southampton beat Manchester United in 1976 and Ipswich Town beat Arsenal in 1978. These were viewed as 'upsets' by the football fraternity - though plenty of people were far from upset - and an explanation was sought. Sports psychology still being in its infancy, words like complacency, incentive and pressure of expectation were ignored and the shock results were put down to the fact that the winning teams had used the same (South) dressing room. Spooky!

This now became the Lucky Dressing Room which everyone wanted. So now on Cup Final Day, the team whose name begins nearest the letter A gets the North (unlucky) Dressing Room. Whoever took that decision was evidently no friend to Arsenal - who have managed to beat the jinx three times since. Is it down to a lucky dressing room? The facts are these: thirteen times the team that changed their shorts in the South Dressing Room have won, eight times the team who disrobed in the North Dressing Room have triumphed. It seems that superstition plays a part in sport and attitude is all.

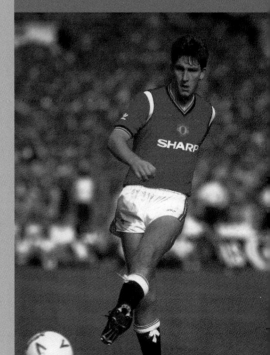

CUP FINAL RECORDS

Most Goals by a Single Player in a Wembley Cup Final STAN MORTENSEN (Blackpool) scored three goals in the famous 'Matthews Final' of 1953.

Youngest Scorer in a Wembley Cup Final NORMAN WHITESIDE (Manchester United) was 18 years 19 days when he helped to defeat Brighton & Hove Albion 4-0 in the replay (held at Wembley) in 1983.

Youngest Captain in a Wembley Cup Final DAVID NISH was only 21 years 212 days old when he captained Leicester City against Manchester City. Sadly, his team lost.

Youngest Player in a Wembley Cup Final PAUL ALLEN was 17 years and 256 days when he played for West Ham United against Arsenal in 1980. West Ham won the trophy.

Record attendance at a Wembley Cup Final The official attendance for the first ever 'White Horse Final' at Wembley 1923 was 126,047, but as everyone knows there were probably double that many there. Although some had tickets, others just paid at the turn-stiles which were some distance from the ground. The stadium had a 120,000 capacity in those days, but much of it was standing room only. Since the stadium became all-seating in 1990, a sold out 80,000 crowd is the norm for a Cup Final these days.

Top Scorer in Wembley Cup Finals IAN RUSH has scored five goals in three Cup Finals (1986, 1989 and 1992), all of them playing for Liverpool. Runner up with four Cup Final goals is Stan Mortensen of Blackpool (1948, 1953). In third place is the distinguished trio of Ian Wright, Eric Cantona and Mark Hughes who have all scored three times in a Cup Final. Wright scored for Crystal Palace in 1990 and Arsenal in 1993, Cantona and Hughes both scored for Manchester United in 1994 and 1996, and 1990 and 1994 respectively.

First Player to Score for Both Teams in a Wembley Cup Final This dubious distinction belongs to BERT TURNER. Playing for Charlton Athletic in the 1946 Final, he scored an own goal for Derby County - this was also the first goal scored in a post-war Cup Final – before equalising a minute later. As if that wasn't enough, the ball burst shortly afterwards!

Seeing Double In the 1931 Final, West Bromwich Albion had two players called Billy Richardson. The centre-half was known as W. RICHARDSON and W. G. RICHARDSON was centre-forward and scorer of Albion's two goals. The 'G' was for Ginger apparently!

Deputy Duty Since 1933 a member of the royal family has presented the Cup to the winning team at Wembley. However, in 1952 the royal family was in mourning for the death of King George VI, so Sir Winston Churchill stood in for the new Queen – the only prime minister ever to do so.

Do It All Over Again In 1970 the first replay ever necessary after a Wembley Cup Final took place at Old Trafford, where Chelsea beat Leeds United. Since then there have been four occasions when a replay match was needed.

Tickets for Teams Following protests from fans about unfair ticket allocation, the two finalist clubs get a larger share of the tickets. The actual allocation is decided by a so-called swing factor – dependant on the average gates over a number of seasons. If teams have an equal gate they get equal allocation, if not it is worked out in proportion. It all comes down to putting bums on seats after all.

Abide With Me The tradition of community singing began at the 1927 Cup Final. The most famous song sung was *Abide With Me*, a Victorian hymn about death, which was introduced at the very first sing-song by the original Man in a White Suit, Thomas P Ratcliff (there have been several). This rather doomy dirge was in contrast to the either jolly (*Tipperary, She'll Be Coming Round The Mountain*) or rousing (*John Brown's Body, Land of My Fathers*) songs which made up the rest of the programme. *Abide With Me* has always had a sobering effect on the crowd and was the last tune before the teams came out of the tunnel.

Pompey and Circumstance Portsmouth held the FA Cup for longer than any other team. They won it in 1939 then war broke out and there were no cup finals until 1946.

Not Amused 1976 was the last year the Queen attended the Cup Final at Wembley. Her Majesty, who is allegedly a lot more interested in horsey sports, endured over two decades of football duty at these events, before handing over the reins, so to speak, to one of her relatives.

above: **High-spirited West Ham fans arriving at Wembley for the first Cup Final ever to be held there.**
below: **Those without tickets scaled the walls of the stadium to be sure of a good view of the action.**

stop press

The last ever AXA sponsored FA Cup Final at Wembley Stadium took place on May 20th 2000. It was a day for remembering great Cup Finals of the past and was a suitably emotional occasion.

Chelsea
the winning team

Ed De Goey

Celestine Babayaro

Frank Leboeuf

Marcel Desailly

Didier Deschamps

Gustavo Poyet

Dennis Wise (captain)

Mario Melchiot

Roberto Di Matteo

Gianfranco Zola

George Weah

SUBS:

Tore Andre Flo

(replaced Weah)

Jody Morris

(replaced Zola)

Manager: Gianluca Vialli

right: **Chelsea heroes Dennis Wise and Roberto Di Matteo.** far right: **Mario Melchiot beats Ian Taylor to the ball.**

Special tickets featured likenesses of eleven historical football heroes and spectators received commemorative pennants. A parade of children representing each of the cup-winning teams was followed by operatic diva Lesley Garrett leading the singing of *Abide With Me*.

Chelsea, with their team of expensive foreign imports, were the favourites, but many felt that Aston Villa were a match for them. In the first half it was anybody's guess as to who would walk off with the trophy, but in the second half, Chelsea began to dominate. Dennis Wise had a goal disallowed, because George Weah was offside, then in the 73rd minute Roberto Di Matteo broke the deadlock with the only goal of the match. In addition to carrying off football's most famous domestic prize, Chelsea, by winning the Cup Final, were automatically awarded a place in the UEFA Cup.

When the final Final was over there were two contrasting images. On the podium was Dennis Wise clutching his proudest possessions, The FA Cup and his baby son Henry, while on the pitch lay David James, the Villa goalie, covering up his face with his jersey to hide his tears. The winner takes it all.

Had Aston Villa won they would have been the first team to win The FA Cup in three different centuries. Three of their seven pre Wembley wins took place in the 19th century (1887, 1895, 1897). Their opponents in the semi-final were Bolton, who won the first Wembley Cup Final. Had Bolton won the penalty shootout instead of Villa they would have had the distinction of being in the first and last Wembley Cup Finals.

CUP FINAL 2000
Chelsea 1 - Aston Villa 0

Roberto Di Matteo entered the Wembley record book for the second time. In addition to his record as the scorer of the fastest goal in a Cup Final (43 seconds in 1997), he became the last man ever to score a goal in an FA Cup Final at Wembley.

The winning team comprised three Frenchmen, two Italians, two Dutchmen, a Norwegian, a Nigerian, a Uruguayan, a Liberian and two Englishmen.

above: **The winning goal goes in the net.** above right: **The official programme strikes a nostalgic note.** below: **Chelsea celebrate after winning the FA Cup Final.**

Aston Villa
the gallant losers

David James
Alan Wright
Gareth Southgate (captain)
Ugo Ehiogu
George Boateng
Ian Taylor
Dion Dublin
Paul Merson
Gareth Barry
Benito Carbone
Mark Delaney

SUBS:

Steve Stone
(replaced Taylor)
Julian Joachim
(replaced Carbone)
Lee Hendrie
(replaced Wright)
Manager: John Gregory

team	won	lost	points
Manchester United	1948,1963,1977,1983,1985,1990,1994, 1996,1999	1957,1958,1976,1979,1995	23
Arsenal	1930,1936,1950,1971,1979,1993,1998	1927,1932,1952,1972, 1978,1980	20
Liverpool	1965,1974,1986,1989,1992	1950,1971,1977,1988,1996	15
Newcastle United	1924,1932,1951,1952,1955	1974,1998,1999	13
Tottenham Hotspur	1961,1962,1967,1981,1982,1991	1987	13
Everton	1933,1966,1984,1995	1968,1985,1986,1989	12
Manchester City	1934,1956,1969	1926,1933,1955,1981	10
Bolton Wanderers	1923,1926,1929,1958	1953	9
Chelsea	1970,1997,2000	1967,1994	8
West Bromwich Albion	1931,1954,1968	1935	7
West Ham United	1964,1975,1980	1923	7
Leeds United	1972	1965,1970,1973	5
Preston North End	1938	1937,1954,1964	5
Sunderland	1937,1973	1992	5
Wolverhampton Wanderers	1949,1960	1939	5
Aston Villa	1957	1924,2000	4
Blackpool	1953	1948,1951	4
Leicester City		1949,1961,1963,1969	4
Portsmouth	1939	1929,1934	4
Sheffield Wednesday	1935	1966,1993	4
Blackburn Rovers	1928	1960	3
Cardiff City	1927	1925	3
Charlton Athletic	1947	1946	3
Huddersfield Town		1928,1930,1938	3
Nottingham Forest	1959	1991	3
Sheffield United	1925	1936	3
Birmingham City		1931,1956	2
Burnley		1947,1962	2
Coventry City	1987		2
Derby County	1946		2
Ipswich Town	1978		2
Southampton	1976		2
Wimbledon	1988		2
Brighton & Hove Albion		1983	1
Crystal Palace		1990	1
Fulham		1975	1
Luton Town		1959	1
Middlesbrough		1997	1
Queens Park Rangers		1982	1
Watford		1984	1

Here we focus on those teams who have made a particular contribution to the story of Wembley Stadium.

deserving a special mention

So many great teams have played in Cup Finals at Wembley. They all deserve credit for obtaining a place in the Final, but lack of space means that only a few of them can be singled out for attention. First we look at The Magnificent Seven – the seven teams who have appeared most often in Wembley Cup Finals – Manchester United, Arsenal, Liverpool, Newcastle United, Tottenham Hotspur, Everton and Manchester City. Bearing in mind the feelings of the fans and players of other clubs, this is not a list of the seven best teams. The choice is made by facts (see the Roll of Honour opposite) not opinion.

As well as the big names who've been to Wembley many times, we feature those teams who have only played one Cup Final at Wembley. They are divided into those who won, The Giantkillers, and those who sadly lost, So Near and Yet So Far. Derby County (1946), Southampton (1976), Ipswich Town (1978), Coventry City (1987), and Wimbledon (1988) went home to a heroes' welcome. Luton Town (1959), Fulham (1975), Queens Park Rangers (1982), Brighton and Hove Albion (1983), Watford (1984), Crystal Palace (1990) and Middlesbrough (1997) all fell at the last fence.

Cup-winning teams

1948	1963 / 1977	1976 / 1983	1979 (REPLAY) / 1985	1983 / 1990	1990	1994	1996	1999
Crompton	Crerand	Pearson	REPLAY	McGrath	Webb	Schmeichel	Schmeichel	Schmeichel
Carey	Foulkes	Macari	Bailey	Moran	McClair	Parker	Irwin	G. Neville
Aston	Setters	Hill	Duxbury	Robson	Hughes	Irwin	P. Neville	P. Neville
Anderson	Giles	SUB	Albiston	Strachen	Wallace	Bruce	May	May
Chilton	Quixall	McCreery	Wilkins	Hughes	SUBS	Kanchelskis	Keane	Keane
Cockburn	Herd		Moran	Stapleton	Blackmore	Pallister	Pallister	Johnsen
Delaney	Law	Bailey	McQueen	Olsen	Robins	Cantona	Cantona	Beckham
Morris	Charlton	Duxbury	Robson	SUB	REPLAY	Ince	Beckham	Scholes
Rowley		Moran	Muhren	Duxbury	Sealey	Keane	Cole	Cole
Pearson	Stepney	McQueen	Stapleton		Ince	Hughes	Butt	Solskjaer
Mitten	Nicholl	Albiston	Whiteside	Leighton	Martin	Giggs	Giggs	Giggs
	Albiston	Davies	Davies	Ince	Bruce	SUBS	SUBS	SUBS
	McIlroy	Wilkins		Martin	Phelan	Sharpe	G. Neville	Sheringham
Gaskell	B.Greenhoff	Robson	Bailey	Bruce	Pallister	McClair	Scholes	Stam
Dunne	Buchan	Muhren	Gidman	Phelan	Robson			Yorke
Cantwell	Coppell	Stapleton	Albiston	Pallister	Webb			
	J.Greenhoff	Whiteside	Whiteside	Robson	McClair			
					Hughes			
					Wallace			

Manchester United

Manchester United's first Wembley Cup Final in 1948 was a triumph: a 4-2 win over Stanley Matthews' Blackpool and a vintage final. United, managed by Matt Busby, played an attacking but entertaining game, with goals from Jack Rowley (2), Pearson and Anderson. Despite their impressive Wembley debut it was a long time before Manchester United played another Cup Final. The Busby Babes, as the young team were known, finally reached the final in 1957 only to lose 1-2 to Aston Villa. United's goalie Ray Wood broke his cheekbone after six minutes and had to come off, leaving the side down to ten men. His place in goal was taken by Jackie Blanchflower, who managed a few good saves. United's only goal was scored by Tommy Taylor, soon to die in the Munich air disaster, along with seven other players. Blanchflower was so badly injured that his career ended.

Next year Manchester United were in the final again, but only two players from the previous year remained in the team (Bobby Charlton and Bill Foulkes). They faced Bolton Wanderers and the country wanted them to win, but it wasn't to be. In 1963 they were back at the top with a 3-1 victory over Leicester City. At the time Leicester City were the favourites and Manchester United were struggling to avoid relegation. Although Denis Law scored one goal and David Herd two, it was considered a one man (Law) final.

United suffered a humiliating defeat in 1976 against Southampton, who were the only side to score. This gave the club an incentive and they won the next year against Liverpool (2-1), with goals by Stuart Pearson and Jimmy Greenhoff. This was a cracking final, with all the goals scored within the space of five minutes just after half time.

the magnificent

Manchester United felt vindicated, especially as they had beaten Southampton in the fifth round. Another 'five minute final' in 1979 against Arsenal was a brilliantly exciting match which ended in defeat for United. With five minutes to go Arsenal were ahead by two goals, then United scored twice to equalise. The stadium erupted. Arsenal took advantage of United's euphoria to slip a goal in and the whistle went.

The 1983 defeat of brave little Brighton began a 12 year run of unbeaten Cup Finals for Manchester United. A 2-2 draw with Brighton and Hove Albion led to a replay on Sir Matt Busby's birthday, which United won 4-0. Frank Stapleton and Ray Wilkins scored in the first match and in the replay Bryan Robson got two goals, Norman Whiteside, at 18 years and 19 days the youngest player to score in a Cup Final, got one and there was a penalty from Arnold Muhren. In 1985 a goal in extra time from Whiteside won them the Cup against Everton (1-0). This match is remembered as the only occasion when a player was sent off in a Cup Final. Kevin Moran was the player concerned and most commentators thought the ref's decision a bit harsh. United still managed to win with only ten men.

The Nineties were Manchester United's golden years, with five Cup Final appearances, four of them wins. Even so Crystal Palace took them to a replay in 1990. The first game was a 3-3 draw (goals by Bryan Robson and Mark Hughes [2]) but the replay was an easy 1-0 victory. In 1994 Alex Ferguson's spending had paid off: Eric Cantona, who had

quickly become a cult figure with the fans, scored two penalties in the final against Chelsea. Manchester United won 4-0, the other goals coming from Mark Hughes and Brian McClair. They also won the Double that year. Next year brought a surprise defeat for the club when Everton beat them in the final. Cantona was not in the team; he was suspended following an incident at Selhurst Park when he had given a spectator a Bruce Lee style kung fu kick.

Cantona was back in the team for the 1996 final against Liverpool, which was won 1-0 with his brilliant goal five minutes from the end. In 1999 Manchester United won against Newcastle United 2-0. It started badly when Roy Keane was injured after nine minutes and Teddy Sheringham was brought on. But within two minutes Sheringham had scored. Many thought that Newcastle were playing better but it was Paul Scholes of Manchester United who scored.

above: Paul Scholes gets a bear hug from Teddy Sheringham after scoring in the 1999 Cup Final.
below: Eric Cantona endures a double piggyback from team-mates after a penalty in the 1994 Final.

seven

WON: 1930, 1936, 1950, 1971, 1979, 1993, 1998

LOST: 1927, 1932, 1952, 1972, 1978, 1980

Cup-winning teams

1930	1936	1950	1971	1979	1993	1993 Smith REPLAY	1998
Preedy	Wilson	Swindin	Wilson	Jennings	Seaman	Seaman	Seaman
Parker	Male	Scott	Rice	Rice	Dixon	Dixon	Dixon
Hapgood	Hapgood	Barnes	McNab	Nelson	Winterburn	Winterburn	Keown
Baker	Crayston	Forbes	Storey	Talbot	Davis	Davis	Adams
Seddon	Roberts	L. Compton	McLintock	O'Leary	Linighan	Linighan	Winterburn
John	Copping	Mercer	Simpson	Young	Adams	Adams	Parlour
Hulme	Hulme	Cox	Armstrong	Brady	Jensen	Jensen	Vieira
Jack	Bowden	Logie	Graham	Sunderland	Wright	Wright	Petit
Lambert	Drake	Goring	Radford	Stapleton	Campbell	Smith	Overmars
James	James	Lewis	Kennedy	Price	Merson	Merson	Wreh
Bastin	Bastin	D. Compton	George	Rix	Parlour	Campbell	Anelka
			SUB	SUB	SUBS	SUB	SUB
			Kelly	Walford	O'Leary	O'Leary	Platt

Arsenal

Arsenal, Arsenal, so good they named a tube station after it. Consistency has made Arsenal a regular at Wembley Cup Finals. They are the only club in the Magnificent Seven to have played all their Cup Finals at Wembley,

the first final being 1927 when they lost to Cardiff City 0-1. Arsenal had recently been taken over by Herbert Chapman and it was under him that they became a significant force in the footballing world.

In 1930 they defeated Huddersfield Town (Chapman's previous team) 2-0, thanks to goals by the great Alex James and Jack Lambert and no thanks to an uninvited *Graf Zeppelin* hovering over the field during the match. Also playing for Arsenal was David Jack, the first man ever to score a goal (for Bolton Wanderers) at Wembley.

In 1932 Arsenal lost to Newcastle 1-2, in a match remembered for the disputed over-the-line goal that gave the Cup, unfairly, it later turned out, to Newcastle. The Gunners were gracious in defeat. In 1936 they beat Sheffield United 1-0, with a goal by Ted Drake, playing with an enormous bandage around his injured leg. Again, there was something in the air that day - this time it was the whirring of helicopters hired by rival companies to film the match.

Alterations to the stadium meant that 100,000 were able to watch the Cup Final in 1950. Arsenal beat Liverpool 2-0, both goals scored by Reg Lewis. Playing for Arsenal were Denis Compton, better known for his outstanding cricketing skills, and his brother Leslie, also a cricketer. At 32 and 38 respectively, they were both a bit past it by today's standards:

Denis had to have a brandy to keep him going at half-time. Those were the days! In 1952 Arsenal were beaten by Newcastle 0-1. Wally Barnes was injured after 35 minutes, so Arsenal had to manage with ten men.

After a lull in the Sixties, Arsenal came back in 1971 to beat Liverpool 2-1, with goals by Eddie Kelly and local boy Charlie George. They were in the final the following year, but lost to Leeds United 0-1. Ipswich Town beat them 1978, but Arsenal got straight back to Wembley with a famous 3-2 victory over Manchester United. It was neck and neck until the last minute when Alan Sunderland scored. Arsenal's other goals were by Talbot and Stapleton. In the final again in 1980, they lost to West Ham United 0-1.

Arsenal won in 1993, beating Sheffield Wednesday 2-1 in the replay after a 1-1 draw. Ian Wright scored in both matches and the other goal was by Andy Linighan. The kick-off to the replay was held up (for the first time since the White Horse Final of 1923) because Wednesday fans had been delayed by an accident on the M1. They won the Double in 1998, defeating Newcastle 2-0. Marc Overmars (Dutch) and Nicolas Anelka (French) scored the goals, and Arsene Wenger (French) managed the team of Eurostars. Recent sides have been so difficult to break down, they've been the one team few want to face at Wembley.

above: We are the champions! The Arsenal team celebrate their 1998 win over Newcastle United. below left: Marc Overmars after scoring the first goal of the 1998 Final. below right: Ian Wright lifts the ball over Sheffield Wednesday's goalkeeper to score in the 1993 replay.

FA Cup Final History

Cup-winning teams

1965	1974	1986	1989	1992
Lawrence	Clemence	Grobbelaar	Grobbelaar	Grobbelaar
Lawler	Smith	Lawrenson	Ablett	R. Jones
Byrne	Lindsay	Beglin	Staunton	Burrows
Strong	Thompson	Nicol	Nicol	Nicol
Yeats	Cormack	Whelan	Whelan	Molby
Stevenson	Hughes	Hansen	Hansen	Wright
Callaghan	Keegan	Dalglish	Beardsley	Saunders
Hunt	Hall	Johnston	Aldridge	Houghton
St. John	Heighway	Rush	Houghton	Rush
Smith	Toshack	Molby	Barnes	McManaman
Thompson	Callaghan	MacDonald	McMahon	Thomas
			SUBS	
			Venison	
			Rush	

Liverpool

Late starters in terms of Wembley Cup Finals (although they were in the 1914 Cup Final), Liverpool's success is a post-war phenomenon. They have won only 50% of their finals, and they began their Wembley run with a

defeat: in 1950 they lost 0-2 to Arsenal. They then had to wait for 15 years to get another shot at the trophy.

It wasn't until the Swinging Sixties, when the city of Liverpool received a tremendous boost from its association with the Beatles, that Liverpool triumphed. In 1965 they beat Leeds United, another rising side, 2-1. By now they were managed by football legend Bill Shankly, the man who, it was said, was more loved by the fans than the players were. Liverpool's goals were scored by Roger Hunt and Ian St. John, future TV pundit. All the goals were scored in extra time. Gerry Byrne played most of the game with a broken collar bone. For the first time Wembley Stadium echoed to the tune of *You'll Never Walk Alone*, a recent hit for Liverpool group Gerry and the Pacemakers. Rodgers and Hammerstein never realised they were creating the ultimate football anthem, when they wrote the song for *Carousel*.

In 1971 Liverpool lost 1-2 to Arsenal, but in 1974 they demolished Newcastle 3-0, with two goals by Kevin Keegan and one by Steve Heighway. Keegan had been bought from Scunthorpe: it looked like money well spent. Although Newcastle played badly – lucky to get nil, the wits said - two players impressed their opponents: Terry McDermott and Alan Kennedy were both playing for Liverpool in their next

Cup Final in 1977. It didn't help though, Liverpool lost 1-2 to Manchester United.

Back on top in the Eighties, Liverpool won 3-1 against Everton. The all-Mersey final was a happy occasion, a thrilling match, with good-humoured rivalry (both sets of supporters travelling down to London together) and no hooliganism. Goals were scored by Ian Rush (2) and Craig Johnston. With Kenny Dalglish as player-manager, Liverpool

won the Double that year. Two years later they were back at Wembley, certain of a win against surprise finalists Wimbledon. The result (0-1) was an Almighty Upset - Liverpool were wombled!

The all-Mersey final of 1989 was a very different affair. It took place less than a month after the Hillsborough Disaster, when 95 Liverpool fans were crushed to death at the semi-final against Nottingham Forest. Many felt that the competition should be scrapped that year and the final cancelled, but eventually it was felt that fans wanted it to go ahead. It was a sombre occasion, made all the more poignant by Gerry Marsden (of Gerry and the Pacemakers) leading the singing of *You'll Never Walk Alone*. Liverpool beat Everton 3-2, with goals by John Aldridge and Ian Rush (2), who came on as a substitute. Everyone felt that Liverpool had earned their win that year.

In 1992 Liverpool beat Sunderland 2-0, with goals by Michael Thomas and Ian Rush. This was Rush's fifth Cup Final goal, a record still unbeaten. For some reason it had been decided that the runners-up should mount the thirty-nine steps first for the presentation instead of the winners, as had been the tradition. A communications failure occurred and Sunderland found themselves being presented with winner's medals by mistake. Although Liverpool were handed the trophy, they got the runners-up medals and had to swap medals with the Sunderland players afterwards.

below: The Liverpool team with the trophy after their victory over Merseyside rivals Everton in 1986.
left: The winning side make a triumphal tour of Liverpool in an open-deck bus.

from left to right: Alan Hansen, captain of the 1986 team; John Aldridge in action at the 1989 Cup Final; Kenny Dalglish celebrating the 1986 win; Liverpool partying on after the trouncing of Everton.

FA Cup Final History

Cup-winning teams

1924	1932	1951	1952	1955
Bradley	McInroy	Fairbrother	Simpson	Simpson
Hampson	Nelson	Cowell	Cowell	Cowell
Hudspeth	Fairhurst	Corbett	McMichael	Batty
Mooney	McKenzie	Harvey	Harvey	Scoular
Spencer	Davidson	Brennan	Brennan	Stokoe
Gibson	Weaver	Crowe	E. Robledo	Casey
Low	Boyd	Walker	Walker	White
Cowan	Richardson	Taylor	Foulkes	Milburn
Harris	Allen	Milburn	Milburn	Keeble
McDonald	McMenemy	G.Robledo	G.Robledo	Hannah
Seymour	Lang	Mitchell	Mitchell	Mitchell

Newcastle United

It is over 40 years since Newcastle United have won the Cup Final, yet in recent years they have reached the final two years running and they're now looking strong under Bobby Robson. In 1924 they played against Aston Villa

and won 2-0. It was a good match on a heavy pitch, neck and neck until Newcastle got two late goals in four minutes. Neil Harris scored one and Stan Seymour - who would serve over 50 years with the club as player, manager, director, chairman and vice-president - scored the other. Another player, Billy Hampson, is in many record books as the oldest player (aged 41) ever in a Wembley Cup Final, but recently his birth certificate came to light, revealing that he was a mere 39 and therefore not the oldest player after all.

In 1932 Newcastle beat Arsenal 2-1. Both goals were by Jack Allen, but the first was a famously disputed over-the-line goal. The ball, whilst in Newcastle's possession, crossed the line before being kicked to Allen who then scored. The referee and the linesman did not see it happen and allowed the goal. Later a Movietone newsreel showed the ball had been out of play, but the referee's decision stood. Arsenal cannot have been happy with the result, but could not be drawn by the press into saying anything petulant. It is hard to imagine such good sportsmanship nowadays.

In 1951 Newcastle defeated Stanley Matthews' Blackpool 2-0. Both goals were by Jackie Milburn. 'Wor Jackie', as he was known on Tyneside, was the uncle of the famous Charlton brothers. Blackpool had had a shot saved right under the crossbar early on in the match, so once again there was a slight feeling that Newcastle were lucky to have won. They became the first club to win two years running at Wembley when they beat Arsenal 1-0 in 1952. The goal was

scored by Chilean George Robledo, whose brother Ted also played. George was involved in the tackle that injured Wally Barnes in the 35th minute. Arsenal played the rest of the game with ten men.

A fifth win in five finals at Wembley occurred in 1955, when Newcastle beat Manchester City 3-1. Jackie Milburn scored after 45 seconds. Newcastle's other goals were by Bobby Mitchell and George Hannah, both in the second half. Yet again Newcastle's opponents were down to ten men by the second half.

Their luck ran out in 1974 when, having made it to the final against Liverpool, they were soundly beaten 0-3, with two of those goals coming from Liverpool's new star, Kevin Keegan. Keegan later played for Newcastle and then became the manager who launched the club's return to form in the Nineties. It briefly looked as though they had the flair and passion to win anything they wanted. In 1998 they were outclassed by the cosmopolitan Arsenal and the following year they failed to get the better of Manchester United, despite playing a team of expensive foreign imports.

above: **Frank Hudspeth with a police escort taking the Cup back to the dressing room after the 1924 win over Aston Villa.** *right:* **Alan Shearer, captain of England and Newcastle United.**

Cup-winning teams

1961	1962	1967	(BOTH GAMES)	SUB (1ST GAME ONLY)		Howells
Brown	Brown	Jennings	Aleksic	Brooke	Archibald	Mabbutt
Baker	Baker	Kinnear	Hughton		Galvin	Stewart
Henry	Henry	Knowles	Miller	1982	Hoddle	Gascoigne
Blanchflower	Blanchflower	Mullery	Roberts	(BOTH GAMES)	Crooks	Samways
Norman	Norman	England	Perryman	Clemence	SUB	Lineker
Mackay	Mackay	Mackay	Villa	Hughton	Brooke	Allen
Jones	Medwin	Robertson	Ardiles	Miller		SUBS
White	White	Greaves	Archibald	Price		Nayim
Smith	Smith	Gilzean	Galvin	Hazard	Thorstvedt	Walsh
Allen	Greaves	Venables	Hoddle	Perryman	Edinburgh	
Dyson	Jones	Saul	Crooks	Roberts	Van Den	
					Hauwe	
					Sedgley	

Tottenham Hotspur

With the highest (85%) winning average in Wembley Cup Finals of our Magnificent Seven, Tottenham Hotspur have a tradition of winning in years ending in a 1. They also won pre-Wembley in 1901 and 1921.

In 1961 Spurs were riding high. They won the League and the FA Cup. Their strong team captained by Danny Blanchflower beat Leicester City 2-0, the goals coming near the end of the game from Bobby Smith and Terry Dyson. Leicester had the young Gordon Banks in goal, but Len Chalmers was injured after only 18 minutes and this was in the days of no substitutions.

Spurs won again in 1962, this time thanks to their new star Jimmy Greaves, who scored only three minutes into the game. They beat Burnley 3-1, the other goals coming from Smith and Blanchflower. 1967 saw the first all-London final when Spurs beat Chelsea 2-1. A comparatively easy match for Spurs, they scored through Jimmy Robertson and Frank Saul, and Chelsea's only goal four minutes from time came too late to affect the result.

In 1981 Spurs were back on top again, tackling Manchester City for the 100th Cup Final. The match ended in a 1-1 draw - both goals having been scored by City's Tommy Hutchison. The first ever Wembley Cup Final Replay took place five days later. It was a better game than the first, closely fought and climaxing with one of Wembley's greatest ever goals. Ricky Villa had been substituted during the first game and was very upset. There were tears in the dressing room and talk of going home to Argentina.

When he was told he would be in the replay, all was forgotten and forgiven and he put in one of the all-time great Wembley performances. Villa scored his first goal in seven minutes, then Manchester City got a couple of goals, Garth Crooks equalised, and finally Villa secured the 3-2 victory with a brilliant defence-dodging run before, as he said, "I introduce the ball in the goal."

Spurs repeated their trick of winning the Cup for two seasons by beating Queens Park Rangers. As before, there was a 1-1 draw on the Saturday, but the replay was unremarkable. Glenn Hoddle scored the only goal of the match - a penalty. He had scored Spurs' goal in the first match too. Ossie

Ardiles and Ricky Villa were unable to play because of the Falklands War, which had just begun. They were missed. In 1987 Spurs surprisingly got beaten in a shock defeat by Coventry City (2-3). Coventry played their socks off but they shouldn't have been able to defeat a team with Ossie Ardiles, Ray Clemence and the rhyming couplet Waddle and Hoddle in it. An own goal in extra time by Gary Mabbutt (who had earlier scored in the right net) was the deciding factor. Spurs' other goal was from Clive Allen.

Tottenham, now managed by former Cup-winning player Terry Venables, came back to Wembley and won in 1991. They beat Brian Clough's Nottingham Forest 2-1, with a goal from Paul Stewart and an own goal from Des Walker in extra time. Things hadn't gone Spurs' way at first. Gary Lineker, of all people, had missed a penalty. Paul Gascoigne was only on the field for 20 minutes, but it is his game that everyone remembers. Even before the kick-off he was acting like he was auditioning for *Men Behaving Badly*. Within minutes he kicked Garry Parker in the chest and, unbelievably, got away with it. Soon afterwards he launched a tackle against Gary Charles, which tore a ligament in his (Gazza's) knee. He should have been sent off, but instead he was stretchered off to hospital and Stuart Pearce was given a free-kick which resulted in Forest's only goal. Gascoigne's injury was long-lasting and the demise of his brilliant career can be traced from that moment.

Gary Lineker holds up the FA Cup after Tottenham beat Nottingham Forest in 1991. above right: **Alan Mullery and Dave Mackay share the honour of holding the trophy after the 1967 win over Chelsea.** left: **Dyson puts one past Gordon Banks of Leicester City in 1961.**

Cup-winning teams

1933	1966	1984	1995	SUBS
				Amokachi
				Ferguson
Sagar	West	Southall	Southall	
Cook	Wright	Stevens	Jackson	
Cresswell	Wilson	Bailey	Ablett	
Britton	Gabriel	Ratcliffe	Parkinson	
White	Labone	Mountfield	Watson	
Thomson	Harris	Reid	Unsworth	
Geldard	Scott	Steven	Limpar	
Dunn	Trebilcock	Heath	Horne	
Dean	Young	Sharp	Stuart	
Johnson	Harvey	Gray	Rideout	
Stein	Temple	Richardson	Hinchcliffe	

Everton

Everton made their first Wembley Cup Final appearance in 1933, but though they were strangers to the venue they had been in Cup Finals in 1893, 1897, 1906 and 1907. 1933 was the heyday of the record-holding

scorer Dixie Dean, and Everton also had a great defender in Warney Cresswell and Ted 'The Boss' Sagar in goal. They easily outclassed Manchester City, beating them 3-0 with goals by Stein, Dean and Dunn. This was the first final where the teams wore numbers on their backs, but instead of each team being numbered 1 to 11, Manchester City were numbered 12-22. Who knows what the psychological impact of being placed second in numerical order was, but it was soon decided to change the system.

Surprisingly, there followed a gap of more than 30 years before the Toffees made it to the final. In 1966 they were back to face Sheffield Wednesday, in a re-run of the War of the Roses. Sheffield were ahead for most of the match, then, in a classic Cup Final moment, a little known player called Mike Trebilcock scored two goals within five minutes to equalise for Everton. Soon afterwards, with only ten minutes to go, a goal from Temple gave the trophy to Everton. Trebilcock was only a reserve player and had been brought on at the last minute to replace Fred Pickering.

When the final whistle blew, two Everton fans ran onto the pitch to embrace Trebilcock. They were swiftly followed by two policemen, who tripped, lost their helmets and ran all over the pitch before they caught them. It took a rugby tackle to fell one of the fans and six policemen to remove him bodily from the field. The spectators enjoyed the Keystone

Kops chase almost as much as the match. The chase appears regularly on TV.

After all this excitement, Everton's return two years later, when they lost 0-1 to West Bromwich Albion, was distinguished only by the number of fouls. There was to be another dry spell, before Everton dominated the Cup Final, playing in it for three years running. In 1984, in the first of these appearances, they beat Watford 2-0 with goals by Graeme Sharp and recent acquisition Andy Gray. Graham Taylor, Watford's manager, disputed Gray's goal, claiming he had headed it out of the goalkeeper's hands, but the ref didn't agree. Everton refused to be dazzled by Watford's showbiz connections and set their minds on winning.

Unfortunately they couldn't repeat this win in their next two finals. In 1985 they lost to Manchester United (0-1) despite United having a man sent off - the first time this had ever happened in a Cup Final. They not only failed to capitalise on this situation, their eleven men failed to stop their opponents from scoring. In 1986, in an all-Mersey final, they lost to their arch-rivals, Liverpool, 1-3. Not even the presence of new signing Gary Lineker, who scored the first goal of the match, was enough to stop Ian Rush at the height of his powers. In 1989 Everton faced Liverpool again. This was the post-Hillsborough Final and it was only right and proper that Liverpool should win in the circumstances.

William Ralph Dean, known to all as Dixie, was Everton's star player in the Twenties and Thirties. Some say he was the greatest centre-forward of them all and certainly his goal scoring record (473 goals in 502 games) is only threatened by Jimmy Greaves. As a teenager he had fractured his skull and also undergone abdominal surgery, yet he managed a 16 year career, which included playing for England.

left The Everton team line up for a victory pose after beating Watford in 1984. *right* A group hug is required after Everton beat Manchester United in 1995. *below* Gary Ablett and Graham Stuart close in on Nicky Butt in the 1995 Final.

Everton bounced back in 1995 with a surprise win over favourites Manchester United. Everton were faced with relegation and Manchester United were on form, but, crucially, lacked Eric Cantona who had been suspended. A shot by Graham Stuart hit the bar, then Paul Rideout scored in the second half. Everton immediately went into defensive mode and stopped United getting anywhere near the goal. Dixie would have been proud of them.

Cup-winning teams

1934	1956	1969
Swift	Trautmann	Dowd
Barnett	Leivers	Book
Dale	Little	Pardoe
Busby	Barnes	Doyle
Cowan	Ewing	Booth
Bray	Paul	Oakes
Toseland	Johnstone	Summerbee
Marshall	Hayes	Bell
Tilson	Revie	Lee
Herd	Dyson	Young
Brook	Clarke	Coleman

Manchester City

Manchester City's inclusion in Wembley's Magnificent Seven may surprise some. Their pre-Second World War success and more recent decline contrasts with the form of their rivals Manchester United. When City met

Bolton Wanderers for the 1926 Cup Final (which they lost 0-1) they had previously beaten the same club in the 1904 Final, held at Crystal Palace. In 1933 they were in the final again but lost to Everton 0-3, despite the presence of future Manchester United manager Matt Busby in the team. Undaunted, they were back the next year to beat Portsmouth (2-1). Both goals were scored by Fred Tilson.

In the Fifties this pattern of being runners up one year and winners the next was repeated: they lost to Newcastle 1-3 in 1955 and beat Birmingham City 3-1 in 1956. The winning goals were scored by Hayes, Dyson and Johnstone. Don Revie (later England manager) played in both games as centre forward and helped to create two of the goals: apparently his inclusion in the side was a last minute replacement for Bill

Spurdle who had had the misfortune of coming out in boils!

1969 was a good time for Manchester City: besides winning the Cup Final against Leicester City 1-0, they had been League Champions in 1968, they won the League Cup and the European Cup Winner's Cup in 1970. The goal that won the Cup Final was scored in the first half by Neil Young, but a brilliant save by Harry Dowd stopped the match from ending in a draw.

1981 was the 100th Cup Final. City started well against Tottenham Hotspur until Tommy Hutchison scored for both sides, resulting in a draw. The replay also looked promising for Manchester City; with only 18 minutes to go they were 2-1 up, when two Spurs goals in the space of five minutes completely changed the picture.

Ex-German paratrooper and prisoner of war Bert Trautmann was a popular goalkeeper. In the 1956 final he broke his neck with 15 minutes of play still to go and played on rather than leave Manchester City with an open goal.

left Bert Trautmann is helped off the field rubbing his painful neck, which later turned out to be broken. He was named player of the year in 1956. **above** An example of Bert Trautmann's acrobatic goalkeeping.

Much of the 1955 game was played with only 10 men on Manchester City's side. Jimmy Meadows injured his knee and couldn't carry on playing. No substitutes were allowed in those days, but Bobby Johnstone still managed to score a goal. Meadows changed into a blazer and grey flannels and watched the second half on the manager's bench.

1946 Derby County

CUP FINAL TEAM
Woodley
Nicholas
Howe
Bullions
Leuty
Musson
Harrison
Carter
Stamps
Doherty
Duncan

The 1946 Cup Final was a particularly memorable occasion as it was the first since the Second World War so rudely interrupted the game.

Many of the spectators were still in uniform and some of the players were still waiting to be demobbed. An air of seriousness overhung the proceedings during the pre-match presentation to King George VI and there were tears during *Abide With Me*, yet the game which took place on the afternoon of April 27th did manage to live up to six years of expectations.

Charlton Athletic had made a couple of appearances in wartime finals and would win the Cup the following year, but for Derby County this was to be a once in a lifetime occasion. The first Cup Final goal after the Second World War was an own goal by Charlton's Bert Turner. As this was five minutes before the end of normal time after 85 minutes of deadlock, this must have been devastating for Turner, but with a remarkable recovery, he equalised immediately, becoming the first man to score for both sides in a Cup Final. While the spectators were getting over the excitement of that, the ball burst. Ironically the referee, E.D.Smith, had been asked what were the chances of the ball bursting during a match on a radio interview broadcast the day before. "A million-to-one," he said dismissively.

The outcome of the match was decided by the fitness of the players after an action packed 90 minutes. Derby's stars were Raich Carter (who had captained Sunderland when they won the Cup in 1937) and Peter Doherty, who scored in extra time. One other player stands out, Jack Stamps, who hadn't excelled during normal time though it was his power-packed kick which burst the ball. In extra time he scored twice, despite having been injured so badly at Dunkirk that he had been told he would never play again.

left: **Derby half back Leon Leuty jumps for the ball against Bert Turner of Charlton Athletic.** below: **Turner forces a corner off Leuty as Derby goalie Vic Woodley tries to catch the ball.**

the giantkillers

1976 Southampton

CUP FINAL TEAM
Turner
Rodrigues
Peach
Holmes
Blyth
Steele
Gilchrist
Channon
Osgood
McCalliog
Stokes

May 1st 1976 was the day second division Southampton defeated the mighty Manchester United 1-0 at Wembley.

Though Southampton had been in the FA Cup Final in 1900 and 1902, they hadn't made much of an impact since and Tommy Docherty and his United team didn't think they had anything to worry about. But this was the game that would separate the men from the boys: Manchester United were a young, dynamic side, but Southampton were a solid crew, managed by Lawrie McMenemy, with years of experience between them.

Everyone thought that if Southampton scored it would be stars like Mick Channon or Peter Osgood who would put the ball in, but it was the unassuming Bobby Stokes who got the only goal of the match. Sponsors had promised a brand new car to the first player to score: Bobby Stokes couldn't drive and had to have lessons.

A year before, Peter Rodrigues had been given a free transfer to Southampton. Now he was captain of the FA Cup Winners and the last one ever to receive the trophy from the Queen. What a turnaround!

With perfect timing, Mick Channon played his testimonial match against Queens Park Rangers two days after the final. Over 50,000 tried to get into the Dell to see the Saints go marching in.

below: The goal that gave Southampton the Cup. United's Alex Stepney stretches but just can't keep it out.

It is the dream of every club to reach the Cup Final, to play at Wembley and to win against a great team. How sweet it is to come onto the field as no-hopers and to leave with the FA Cup. Here we salute the five teams who had just one day in the sun.

1978 Ipswich Town

CUP FINAL TEAM
Cooper
Burley
Talbot
Hunter
Beattie
Osborne
Mariner
Geddis
Woods
Mills
Wark
SUB
Lambert
(REPLACED ROGER OSBORNE)

Ipswich's only Cup Final appearance at Wembley was a very special day – and not just for Ipswich's impeccably behaved fans.

May 6th 1978 was the 50th Wembley Cup Final and it was appropriate that it should be special. A crowd of 100,000 saw the favourites, Arsenal, outclassed by Wembley virgins. Ipswich, who were managed by future England manager Bobby Robson, had reached the semi-final in 1975 and had a strong side.

The FA tournament was going through an exciting, unpredictable phase: in the 1977-8 season six non-League clubs had reached the third round, and Blyth Spartans got through to the fifth round. Ipswich Town came to the Final with nothing to lose and their 1-0 win was a popular result.

From the word go it was Ipswich's game. Cheered on by their ecstatic sup-porters, decked out in blue and white, they had several near-misses before Roger Osborne hammered the ball home past Pat Jennings in the 77th minute. Local boy Osborne was so overcome with emotion and exhaustion that he collapsed and Mick Lambert was sent on as a substitute.

Mick Mills received the trophy from Princess Alexandra and Ipswich went home to Portman Road for the tradi-tional hero's welcome, complete with open-topped bus, civic reception and an estimated 100,000 lining the streets. Two days later Mick Lambert had his testimonial against an All Star XI and benefited from the 17,000 who came to see the new cup holders.

below Left: **John Wark of Ipswich Town in action.** below right: **Captain Mick Mills led his team to a very popular victory.**

1987 Coventry City

CUP FINAL TEAM
Ogrizovic
Phillips
Downs
McGrath
Kilcline
Peake
Bennett
Gynn
Regis
Houchen
Pickering

SUB
Rodger

(REPLACED KILCLINE)

Coventry City Football Club was in its 104th year, never having set the world on fire, when it finally got to Wembley on May 16th 1987 for the Cup Final,

beating strong teams like Bolton Wanderers, Manchester United, Stoke City, Sheffield Wednesday and Leeds United on their way. They faced Tottenham Hotspur, who had won five times out of five before, and couldn't have had a worse start when Spurs scored within two minutes of kick-off. With nothing to lose they kept their spirits up and twice drew level with Spurs, pushing the game into extra time, before an own goal from Gary Mabbutt gave Coventry the Cup.

Whilst the Spurs line-up included future England manager Glenn Hoddle, Chris Waddle and Ossie Ardiles, Coventry's side was solid but without stars. Keith Houchen, whose spectacular header was Coventry's second equaliser - Dave Bennett scored the first - had been playing in the fourth division (for Scunthorpe United) the previous year.

Once again the underdogs had beaten the odds and sent the favourites home empty-handed.

below left: **Goal-scorer Dave Bennett holds the trophy aloft for the fans.**
below right: **Bennett takes on Gary Mabbutt for possession of the ball.**

1988 Wimbledon

CUP FINAL TEAM
Beasant
Goodyear
Phelan
Jones
Young
Thorn
Gibson
Cork
Fashanu
Sanchez
Wise

SUBS
Scales

(REPLACED GIBSON)

Cunningham

(REPLACED CORK)

Of all the giantkillers, the story of Wimbledon's defeat of the mighty Liverpool on May 14th 1988 is probably the most legendary.

Described as a 'custard pie in the face of predictability' and 'the Crazy Gang (beating) the Culture Club', it was not the greatest match ever. When Liverpool won their first final in 1965, Wimbledon were still a bunch of part-timers, a dozen years away from membership of the Football League. On their way up they gained a reputation which later earned them the nickname 'the Crazy Gang'. Everyone was looking forward to the hardest of their hard men, Vinnie Jones, meeting Liverpool's tough guy Steve McMahon.

Fortune smiled on Wimbledon when the referee disallowed a goal from Peter Beardsley and instead took play back giving Liverpool a free kick. Less than two minutes later a header from Lawrie Sanchez was in the net and Wimbledon were 1-0 up.

In the second half, the Dons' goalie Dave Beasant, who was also the captain, saved a penalty. This was the first time a penalty was missed in a Cup Final, but perhaps it was also the first time a giant was in the goal – Beasant was 6ft 4in. When Wimbledon won 1-0, Beasant was the first goalkeeper to receive the Cup.

When Wimbledon went home for the traditional Cup-winners' welcome 25,000 turned out to cheer them. Sadly, attendance at their matches was never as high as 25,000. Three years later they had to leave Plough Lane, their ground for 79 years, to share Selhurst Park with Crystal Palace.

below left: Wimbledon goalkeeper and captain Dave Beasant and team-mate Alan Cork congratulate each other after the match. **below right:** Vinnie Jones shows off the trophy to the fans who thronged the streets of Wimbledon for their homecoming.

Baynham
McNally
Hawkes
Groves
Owen
Pacey
Bingham
Brown
Morton
Cummins
Gregory

May 2nd 1959 was a great day for Luton Town. They played Nottingham Forest before a crowd of 100,000 at Wembley, put up a good fight and Dave Pacey scored a goal. However, Forest, managed by Billy Walker, who had helped Aston Villa win the FA Cup in 1920 (as a player) and Sheffield Wednesday in 1935 (as Manager), were the better team and they won 2-1.

The match is remembered today because Nottingham Forest became the first team to win with only ten men. Roy Dwight (uncle of Sir Elton John) was carried off on a stretcher after half-an-hour. He had already scored and so had Tommy Wilson (also for Forest), but he broke a leg in a tackle. This was a disaster for Nottingham Forest as no substitutes were allowed in those days. The incident led to much debate on the fairness of allowing substitutions.

They had played so well in the first 13 minutes that they were two goals up, so they concentrated on stopping Luton Town from scoring. Despite the spirited defence Luton managed to score once, a small victory in itself under the circumstances, but it wasn't enough.

Luton

below: Luton's Ron Baynham saves from Roy Dwight's kick. Minutes later Dwight broke his leg.

so near yet so far

Seven clubs have battled their way through the FA Cup to reach the final at Wembley, only to see their dream snatched from them at the last minute. On the day they lost, but they are not losers. To be a Wembley finalist is a great achievement in itself and the highlight of any club's history.

1975 Cup Final Team

Mellor
Cutbush
Lacy
Moore
Fraser
Mullery
Conway
Slough
Mitchell
Busby
Barrett

Not one of the greatest Cup Finals, the meeting of Fulham with West Ham on May 3rd 1975 is memorable as Bobby Moore's swansong. Fulham were in the second division and West Ham had finished 13th in the First Division, so nobody was expecting much from the all-London final - correctly, as it turned out.

There isn't much to say about the actual game. West Ham won 2-0. Both goals were scored by Alan Taylor, aka the Rochdale Whippet, 21 years old, only a few months out of the fourth division and on a run of scoring two goals in every match.

For Fulham, who had made it to the semi-finals twice before, it was a massive thrill. Having the World Cup winning, former England captain playing with them was a tremendous morale boost for the other players. Moore had played for West Ham for 14 years, his best years. Now he was on the edge of retirement. He was as surprised as anyone to find himself back at Wembley for the Cup Final. To be playing against his old team took the biscuit. Some players would have felt pressure to beat his old side - had it been the plot of a Hollywood movie that is what would have happened - but real life is full of disappointments and this was one. The hero of 1966 didn't let it ruin his day, posing for press pictures made up as an old codger and enjoying the pre and post match celebrations to the full. Not a classic Cup Final, but Wembley's last chance to see a classic footballer in action.

Fulham

below: Fulham's loss was West Ham's gain. The winners celebrate their Cup Final victory.

Hucker
Fenwick
Gillard
Waddock
Hazell
Roeder
Currie
Flanagan
Allen
Stainrod
Gregory
SUB
Micklewhite
(REPLACED ALLEN)

Queens Park Rangers

A lthough second division Queens Park Rangers only appeared in one Cup Final – in 1982 – they had the honour of playing in a Wembley Cup Final twice: the first match on May 22nd ended in a 1-1 draw, so there was a rematch, also at Wembley on May 27th. Although it was a midweek match, the all-London replay drew a crowd of 90,000.

Tottenham Hotspur were on a roll. It was their centenary year and they had won the Cup the previous year, their sixth win in six finals. Obviously they were favourites to win, so it came as a shock when Terry Fenwick scored for QPR in extra time, equalising Glenn Hoddle's goal in normal time. Spurs must have felt a chill of fear during the five-day interval. They were without their Argentinian stars, Ossie Ardiles and Ricky Villa, thanks to the Falklands War. Villa had scored two of their three goals against Manchester City in the previous year's final. Now all hopes were pinned on Glenn Hoddle to hang on to the Cup. There was no need to worry; Hoddle delivered with a penalty (awarded when Currie fouled Roberts only six minutes into the game) and the trophy went back to White Hart Lane.

QPR were managed by Terry Venables, who had been a player for Tottenham and had been on the winning team in the 1967 Cup Final. In the 1990s he would of course become England coach.

Replay Team
Hucker
Fenwick
Gillard
Waddock
Hazell
Neill
Currie
Flanagan
Micklewhite
Stainrod
Gregory
SUB
Burke
(REPLACED MICKLEWHITE)

above: QPR watch with relief as Spurs' free kick goes wide. left: Glenn Roeder clears a Spurs corner in the first match.

For the third year running the Cup Final ended in a draw and needed a replay. Thus Brighton and Hove Albion, Wembley novices, were suddenly appearing there twice in a week. The task they faced couldn't have been harder - to defeat the mighty Manchester United. To have held the favourites to a 2-2 draw on May 21st was a fantastic achievement for the Seagulls. Brighton's two goals were scored by Gordon Smith and Gary Stevens.

Yet it was so nearly a victory. In the last minute of extra time Smith had the perfect chance to score and he missed. It was 2-2 and had he scored the game would have been over. The BBC radio commentator uttered the famous words "And Smith must score!" except, of course, he didn't. It was virtually an open goal, but somehow the pressure of the occasion got to Smith and he blew it.

Sadly the replay was not a close contest and Brighton went down 4-0. United had had a scare on the Saturday and they were determined not to let some little south coast club get the better of them on Sir Matt Busby's birthday.

Brighton, led by the colourful Jimmy Melia, had had a funny old year that season. They were relegated from the first division, despite beating Newcastle United, Manchester City, Liverpool, Norwich City and Sheffield Wednesday on their way to Wembley. Their captain, Steve Foster, was unable to take part in the first match due to a suspension. He threatened to go to court over it but did play in the replay on May 26th. Sadly Brighton's fortunes have since declined and in 1997 their beloved Goldstone Ground was razed and turned into a Toys R Us.

Moseley
Ramsey
Stevens
Gatting
Pearce
Smillie
Case
Grealish
Howlett
Robinson
Smith
SUB
Ryan
(REPLACED RAMSEY)

Brighton & Hove Albion

Replay Team
Moseley
Gatting
Pearce
Grealish
Foster
Stevens
Case
Howlett
Robinson
Smith
Smillie
SUB
Ryan
(REPLACED PEARCE)

left: **Jimmy Case of Brighton and Hove Albion tackles Manchester United's Ray Wilkins in the first match.**

Sherwood
Bardsley
Barnes
Callaghan
Jackett
Johnston
Price
Reilly
Sinnott
Taylor
Terry
SUB
Atkinson
(REPLACED PRICE)

Watford

Watford's rise from the Fourth Division to a Wembley Cup Final on May 19th 1984 can be explained in two words – Elton and John. With no disrespect to the players, the club's fortunes took a dramatic turnaround when the millionaire superstar decided to buy the club he had supported since childhood. Graham Taylor, future manager of England, was put in charge and the Yellow Brick Road from Vicarage Road to Wembley was mapped out. Not only was there now money to buy in talent, the boost to the team spirit of having a celebrity chairman was incalculable. Watford were on a roll.

Getting to Wembley was the Hornets' principal goal. Some of the players were overcome with emotion during *Abide With Me*. Everton, their opponents, had their own agenda and were sure they would win that day – and they did, 2-0. Watford were not happy with the result: the second goal, scored by Andy Gray, was thought (though not by the ref) to have been headed out of Watford goalie Steve Sherwood's hands. Elton shed a tear or two, but win or lose, it was a great day for Watford.

above: **David Bardsley fails to stop Everton's Kevin Richardson.** left: **Neil Price of Watford and Graeme Sharp of Everton chase the ball.** right: **John Barnes heading for glory.**

May 12th 1990 saw the first all-seated Cup Final at Wembley. From now on a capacity crowd would mean only 80,000. Crystal Palace were newly promoted and finished the season behind their Cup Final opponents Manchester United only on goal difference. Everyone expected a cracker. And they certainly got it.

Crystal Palace led for the first hour with a header from Gary O'Reilly. Mark Hughes equalised, then Bryan Robson took Man United ahead. Finally Ian Wright was allowed off the substitutes' bench and immediately scored. In extra time Wright scored again, but so did Hughes, which took the game to a replay.

The first match had been brilliant, but as so often happens, the replay on May 17th was a letdown. Crystal Palace had no more to give and let Manchester United take the trophy. Inexplicably Ian Wright was once more on the subs' bench at the start of the game. He had broken his leg twice and was supposedly still recuperating, but even with a dodgy leg he could score a goal out of nothing and he really fired up the team. When he was called on it was too late. Palace lost 0-1.

Martyn
Pemberton
Shaw
Gray
O'Reilly
Thorn
Barber
Thomas
Bright
Salako
Pardew
SUBS
Madden
(REPLACED GRAY)
Wright
(REPLACED BARBER)

Crystal Palace

Replay Team
Martyn
Pemberton
Shaw
Gray
O'Reilly
Thorn
Barber
Thomas
Bright
Salako
Pardew
SUBS
Wright
(REPLACED BARBER)
Madden
(REPLACED SALAKO)

top: **Crystal Palace supporters cheer their team on.** above: **Alan Pardew is held off the ball by Bryan Robson in the first match.**

1997

Cup Final Team

Roberts
Blackmore
Pearson
Festa
Fleming
Stamp
Emerson
Mustoe
Hignett
Juninho
Ravanelli

SUBS

Beck
(REPLACED RAVANELLI)

Vickers
(REPLACED MUSTOE)

Kinder
(REPLACED HIGNETT)

Middlesbrough

This most exotic Cup Final took place on May 17th 1997. Middlesbrough and Chelsea fielded Italians, Brazilians, a Frenchman, a Romanian, a Dane, a Norwegian, a Slovak and a Dutch manager (Ruud Gullit). Before the match was 43 seconds old, one of the Italians, Chelsea's Roberto Di Matteo had scored and broken the record (by two seconds) for quickest goal in a Cup Final. If ever a match was won in the first minute, this was it. Then two key players (Mustoe and Ravanelli) were injured and had to come off. By the time Chelsea scored their second goal courtesy of Eddie Newton, still in the first half, Middlesbrough knew they weren't going to make it.

Managed by former England player and Cup-Final winner Bryan Robson, who felt frustrated sitting on the manager's bench instead of being on the field, Middlesbrough had already lost the League Cup Final and been relegated after the briefest of careers in the Premiership. Talk about pipped at the post.

On their way to Wembley they had also had a potentially giantkilling confrontation where they were the giants: they very nearly lost the semi-final to second division Chesterfield. However, being at Wembley as a finalist was reward in itself, and with around £850,000 as their share of gate receipts they must have cried all the way to the bank. Eleven years earlier the club had gone into liquidation after being relegated to the Third Division, only to be saved, promoted and relegated several times before some big spending bought Boro a ticket to Wembley.

above left: **Gianfranco Zola jumps over Steve Vickers.** above: **Frank Sinclair holds back Fabrizio Ravanelli.**

over the moon

Sunderland became the first side not in the First Division to win the Cup Final at Wembley when they beat Leeds United 1-0 in 1973. It was very much a David and Goliath situation as the Leeds United side comprised 11 full internationals and had been a powerful First Division side for several years. Ian Porterfield scored the only goal of the match, but the hero of the hour was goalie Jim Montgomery, who seemingly grew telescopic arms for an extraordinary and, according to eye-witnesses, anatomically impossible, double save. Sunderland got another shot at the Cup in 1992, but Liverpool soon put paid to that winning 2-0.

Wembley historians always single out the 1953 Cup Final, known to all as The Matthews Final, as one of the greatest games ever at Wembley. Bolton Wanderers were 3-1 up with half an hour to go when Stanley Matthews made it third time lucky for Blackpool. He turned his opponent's defence upside down and set up Blackpool's three late goals. Matthews, known as the Wizard of Dribble, was 38 at the time and had been playing for over 20 years, but this was his first and only Cup Winner's Medal.

The League Cup Final between Arsenal and Swindon Town in 1969 is still remembered in Swindon for the two extra-time goals by Don Rogers, which won the Cup for the Third Division team, despite a pitch turned into a quagmire by the Royal International Horse Show. The underdogs won the match thanks to real flair against an experienced side.

below: Stanley Matthews receives his FA Cup-winner's medal from the Queen after the 1953 Matthews Final

Lowlights
foul ups, flare ups, etc.

In 1927 the FA Cup left England for the first and only time when Cardiff beat Arsenal 1-0. Ironically it was a bungled save by Arsenal's Welsh goalkeeper that turned what would have been a miss into a goal for Cardiff. That must have taken some explaining after the match!

sick as a parrot

The following have been sent off at Wembley:

Boris Stankovic, Yugoslavia v Sweden (Olympic Games Final), 1948.

Antonio Rattin, Argentina v England (World Cup quarter-finals), 1966.

Billy Bremner (Leeds) & **Kevin Keegan** (Liverpool), Charity Shield, 1974.

Gilbert Dresch, Luxembourg v England (World Cup qualifier), 1977.

Kevin Moran, Manchester v Everton (Cup Final), 1985.

Mike Henry, Sudbury Town v Tamworth (FA Vase), 1989.

Jason Cook, Colchester United v Witton Albion (FA Vase), 1992.

Lee Dixon, Arsenal v Tottenham Hotspur (FA Cup semi-final), 1993.

Peter Swan, Port Vale v WBA (play-offs), 1993.

Andrei Kanchelskis, Manchester United v Aston Villa (Coca Cola Cup Final), 1994.

Michael Wallace & Chris Beaumont, Stockport County v Burnley (play-offs), 1994.

Tetsuji Hasiratani, Japan v England (Umbro Cup), 1995.

Derek Ward, Northwich Victoria v Macclesfield Town (FA Trophy), 1996.

Tony Rogers, Dagenham and Redbridge v Woking (FA Trophy), 1997.

Brian Statham, Brentford v Crewe Alexandra (play-offs), 1998.

Carpucho, Portugal v England (Friendly), 1998.

Justin Edinburgh, Tottenham Hotspur v Leicester City (Worthington Cup Final), 1999.

Paul Scholes, England v Sweden (European qualifier), 1999.

Clint Hill, Tranmere Rovers v Leicester City (Worthington Cup Final), 2000.

Mark Delaney, Aston Villa v Bolton Wanderers (FA Cup semi-final), 2000.

above: **Arsenal and Cardiff captains shake hands in 1927.**

England's self-esteem took a battering on October 17th 1973 when they failed to beat Poland to qualify for the 1974 World Cup. It was unthinkable that the victors of 1966 would not even get into the competition but that is what happened. England needed to win, but they could only manage a 1-1 draw, thanks to several amazing saves by the Polish goalie, Tomaszewski. Poland went through instead and eventually came third.

Bad boy/genius Paul Gascoigne may only have escaped being sent off during the Spurs v Nottingham Forest Cup Final (1991) by being stretchered off instead. Even before

play began his behaviour had been 'unusual' to say the least – being boisterous and too familiar with royalty, and trying to knock the bandsmen's hats off as they marched onto the pitch. Practically as soon as the game started he got away with an unnecessarily rough tackle on Garry Parker. A quarter of an hour later he inexplicably fouled Gary Charles, which resulted in a free-kick goal for Forest and a year out of the game with a knee injury for Gascoigne. Spurs managed to win without him and Gascoigne's winner's medal for only 20 minutes play remains his only English honour. Had he been booked for the first offence, things might've been different.

the world

Wembley has been the scene of countless international games, both in competitions and friendlies, and is revered by players and fans throughout the world. In addition to the memorable 1966 World Cup Final and the 1996 European Championship, Wembley has staged five European Cup Finals (1963, 1968, 1971, 1978 and 1992), and two Cup-Winners Cup Finals (1965 and 1993).

● The holder of the record number of goals in any World Cup Final is still **Geoff Hurst** with his hat trick at Wembley in 1966.

● England's biggest win ever at Wembley was in 1982 in a European Championship qualifier against Luxembourg; **England 9, Luxembourg 0.**

● The record for most goals by one player in a single International match at Wembley is held by **Malcolm Macdonald,** who scored five goals for England against Cyprus in 1975.

Wem

comes to

hlev

November 25th 1953, when Hungary beat England 6-3, a date that Wembley Stadium might prefer to forget.

ENGLAND

Merrick, Ramsey, Eckersley, Wright, Johnston, Dickinson, Matthews, Taylor, Mortensen, Sewell, Robb.

HUNGARY

Grosics, Buzanszky, Lorant, Lantos, Bozsik, Zakarias, Budai, Kocsis, Hidegkuti, Puskas, Czibor.

above: **England's triumph.** right: **The World Cup Squad.** top row l-r: **Shepherdson (trainer), Stiles, Hunt, Banks, J. Charlton, Cohen, Wilson, Ramsey (manager).** bottom row: **Peters, Hurst, Moore, Ball, B. Charlton.**

It was a national humiliation and a mega wake-up call for England's players and management. Looking back it is not such a surprise: the Hungarians had won the Olympic Games the year before and for weeks before they arrived the Press were full of how unbeatable they were. They were in the midst of a remarkable run of success - they lost just one game between 1950 and 1956 - which only came to an end when the Soviet tanks rolled in. The Magical Magyars included goalie Gyula Grosics, right half Jozsef Bozsik and the inside forward trio Sandor Kocsis, Nandor Hidegkuti and Ferenc Puskas.

England had never been beaten on home soil by a foreign side. It was Coronation Year and although life in Fifties Britain was pretty grim there were still many people who believed that Britain ruled the world. This out of date, imperialist pride was riding for a fall. And that is what it got

Despite the presence of legends like Billy Wright, Stanley Matthews and Alf Ramsey and the support of a capacity home crowd, Hungary scored within 90 seconds of kick-off. Later in the match the Hungarians scored three goals in the space of seven minutes. The most celebrated of their six goals was a left footer by the captain, Ferenc Puskas, which must rank in everyone's Top Ten Goals of All Time. "They hit us for six," quipped Stanley Matthews.

THE AGONY...

England had to wait over a decade to wipe the bitter taste of defeat from their mouths, but it was worth the wait.

By 1966 England was swinging, they'd never had it so good and Alf Ramsey was demonstrating the power of positive thinking: when he took over managing the England side in 1963, he announced that England would win the World Cup in '66. No ifs or buts. Plenty privately thought he was crazy to leave himself a hostage to fortune, but his single-minded attitude established that this took priority over everything else. The team was carefully picked well in advance and built a tremendous camaraderie and team spirit.

The nation was thoroughly overexcited by July when the tournament began. As England made its way through the heats it became apparent that if they made it to the finals they would meet West Germany (as it then was) at Wembley for the Final. Twenty-one years after the end of the Second World War, still remarkably fresh in the memory of all those over 30, and long before the English learned to sublimate their feelings into complaining about

beach towels around the pool at dawn, there was no way they could let the Germans win.

When the grudge match took place on July 30th, the country was in hysteria in case the unthinkable happened. When Germany equalised in the last seconds of the game England's heart was in its mouth. The excitement of the first 90 minutes was nothing compared to the Extra Time. An exhausted Geoff Hurst scored two goals, one of them the controversial underside of the bar goal. According to legend it had been cloudy, but now the sun came out.

When the BBC's Kenneth Wolstenholme uttered his famous remark "They think it's all over...it is now!", Wembley Stadium erupted in a tidal wave of emotion, both on and off the pitch, tears, hugs, kisses, cartwheels, dancing and singing. Who knows what foreigners made of *EE AY ADDIO*, but anyone who thinks Englishmen have a problem expressing their feelings couldn't have been there.

ENGLAND
Banks, Cohen, J.Charlton, Moore, Wilson, Stiles, B.Charlton, Ball, Hurst, Hunt, Peters.

WEST GERMANY
Tilkowski, Hoettges, Schultz, Weber, Schnellinger, Beckenbauer, Haller, Overath, Seeler, Held, Emmerich.

right: England on their lap of honour with the Jules Rimet Trophy. (l-r) Banks, Wilson, Ball, Charlton, Moore and Cohen.
below: Puskas, the Hungarian captain.

& THE ECSTASY

World Cup

The summer of 1966 saw the greatest event in British sporting history when England hosted and won the World Cup at Wembley Stadium.

above: **Billy Wright, the England skipper, exchanges souvenirs with the US captain before England's humiliating defeat in the 1950 World Cup.**

The Jules Rimet Trophy is named after the president of FIFA, who set up the World Cup competition. The idea for an international championship had been around for ages, but nothing happened until after the First World War when Monsieur Rimet was out for a walk one day in Paris. He had a chance meeting with an Uruguayan diplomat, Enrique Buero, whom he had last seen at the 1924 Olympic Games football tournament in Paris. One thing led to another, and before either of them could say

"Another round, garcon, s'il vous plait", they had organised the first ever World Cup.

Uruguay would be celebrating its centenary in 1930 and were keen to be the host, even though that would mean footing the bill. Most of the other members of FIFA thought this was a seriously bad idea - Uruguay was a three week boat ride away from Europe in those days. However, Rimet and Buero got their way in the end and the first World Cup competition took place in Uruguay. Italy, Spain and Hungary

stayed home and sulked because they couldn't host it. England wasn't there either because they had withdrawn from FIFA years before, amidst much bitterness, over the crucial issue of broken time payments for amateurs. Nevertheless, the most popular sports contest in the world had been established and Uruguay had the distinction of being the first winners as well as the first host nation.

Four years later, Mussolini's Italy hosted – and won - the competition, but Uruguay stayed away. The only World Cup winners not to defend their title, they were offended by the Europeans' reluctance to come to Uruguay in 1930. There was another transatlantic tiff surrounding the 1938 World Cup. Argentina thought that a South American country like them should host it. When France was chosen they boycotted the competition, along with many other American nations. If France was expecting to win as hosts, they were in for a disappointment and they went out of the contest in the quarter-finals. Italy won again.

For 12 years the horror and disrup-tion of the Second World War and its aftermath kept the World Cup out of everyone's minds. The tenacious Jules Rimet, still president of FIFA, suppos-edly hid the trophy under his bed to keep it safe during the war. In 1950 Brazil played host but Uruguay won. This tournament was the first time that England had played in the World Cup: Stanley Matthews, at the peak of his form, was mysteriously not picked and, needless to say, England did not do well, suffering the ultimate humiliation - a defeat at the hands of the USA.

Switzerland did the honours in 1954, with West Germany beating Hungary in the final. Hungary had been expected to win but their star player, Ferenc Puskas, injured his ankle in an earlier match and was not quite up to scratch. In 1958 the World Cup stayed in Europe as Sweden staged the compe-tition, which Brazil won, becoming the first side to win the trophy on a differ-ent continent. Amongst the Brazilians was a teenager called Pele, already an astonishing player and soon to become the most famous Brazilian in the world. This was the start of the Brazilian dom-ination of the World Cup and it was also the first World Cup to be televised. Brazil won again in Chile in 1962, this time without Pele. It was a World Cup marred by violence, especially in the 'Battle of Santiago', otherwise known as Chile v Italy.

above: **The victorious Brazilian team after they beat Sweden to win the 1958 World Cup.** left: **Zito of Brazil jumps for joy in the 1962 Final.**

Sir Stanley Rous, President of FIFA, was quoted in the press on how much the Queen had enjoyed the Final. "The Queen enjoyed it enormously and was thrilled during the final part of extra time. She kept asking 'How much longer to go?'." Did she have a pressing engagement at the Palace or was she trans-fixed by the football?

above left: **Rattin of Argentina is sent off at the quarter-finals.** centre: **Mazurkieviez of Uruguay pushes the ball over the bar in England's opening match.** right: **Pickles the wonder dog.**

When the Italian team arrived home in 1966, after their worst ever World Cup – they were beaten by North Korea and the Soviet Union in the first round – they were pelted with rotten fruit by their disgusted fans.

The historical background to the 1966 World Cup involved some great football and a lot of petty politics. The England versus Germany rivalry even extended to the choosing of a host nation. Germany had also made a bid at the 1960 FIFA Congress to stage the finals, but England was selected instead. By now the World Cup was the premier sporting competition throughout the world and some 70 countries entered the qualifying rounds. The final 16 who played in England were:

Group 1
England, France, Mexico, Uruguay.
Group 2
Argentina, Spain, Switzerland, West Germany.
Group 3
Brazil, Bulgaria, Hungary, Portugal.
Group 4
Chile, Italy, North Korea, Soviet Union.

Before the tournament started, an element of farce was introduced by the theft of the trophy. The thief was never caught; whether it was a prank or whether some intellectually challenged burglar actually thought it could be fenced we will never know. Fortunately it was found a few weeks later lying under a hedge in Beulah Hill, South London, by a dog called Pickles.

Despite an unpromising debut (a goal-less draw with Uruguay), England made it safely through the first round. With hindsight, the most significant features of the first round were Jimmy Greaves' leg injury, which opened the way for Geoff Hurst into the team, and defending champions Brazil losing to Hungary and Portugal.

The quarter-finals saw England against Argentina, West Germany against Uruguay, Portugal against North Korea, and the Soviet Union against Hungary. England's match with Argentina was notable for its rough play. Argentina's captain was sent off because he challenged the referee's authority. Afterwards he claimed that the ref was biased in England's favour, which seems unlikely as the ref was German. There had been a drama behind the scenes too: the FA Board demanded that Alf Ramsey leave Nobby Stiles out of the game. Ramsey steadfastly refused and threatened to resign over it, so the FA backed down.

With the South Americans on their way home, it was an all-European semi-final; West Germany against the Soviet Union and England against Portugal. The England v Portugal match was perhaps Bobby Charlton's finest hour. He scored both of England's goals, the second of which was so sweet that several Portuguese players shook his hand as he walked back to the centre circle. Alf Ramsey's faith in Nobby Stiles paid off; Stiles marked Eusebio, Portugal's star player, so effectively that the only goal he scored was a penalty.

At last the moment Ramsey had dreamed of – England had got to the World Cup finals on their own merits and were about to face the team that considered itself, with some justifica-

"Where were you when Hurst scored his third?" has been a favourite conversational gambit in pubs ever since. Geoff Hurst claims that he has been asked this question himself!

tion, the best in Europe, if not the world. The team would be the same players that had performed so well against Portugal. Jimmy Greaves was fit and, as one of England's ace strikers, expecting to be picked. Ramsey's decision to use Geoff Hurst instead was a devastating blow to Greaves, but turned out well for England. The German manager, Helmut Schoen, had seen how Eusebio had been neutralised by Stiles' marking and decided that Bobby Charlton should be prevented from scoring in the same way. His mistake was choosing Franz Beckenbauer to waste his talents tracking Charlton. Both players spent most of the match dancing round each other.

The atmosphere at Wembley reached new levels of superlatives. 96,000 thronged into the stadium, but thousands lined the route to Wembley just to salute the team. An estimated 600 million people watched the game on television or heard it on the radio. England had been completely taken over by World Cup Fever. Two hours of heart-stopping action and the World Cup was England's. The dream had come true and nothing short of another World War ending could have summoned such national euphoria.

The England World Cup Squad

1.	G. Banks (gk)	Leicester City
2.	G. Cohen	Fulham
3.	R. Wilson	Everton
4.	N. Stiles	Manchester United
5.	J. Charlton	Leeds United
6.	B. Moore	West Ham United
7.	A. Ball	Blackpool
8.	J. Greaves	Tottenham Hotspur
9.	B. Charlton	Manchester United
10.	G. Hurst	West Ham United
11.	J. Connelly	Manchester United
12.	R. Springett (gk)	Sheffield Wednesday
13.	P. Bonetti (gk)	Chelsea
14.	J. Armfield	Blackpool
15.	G. Byrne	Liverpool
16.	M. Peters	West Ham United
17.	R. Flowers	Wolves
18.	N. Hunter	Leeds United
19.	T. Paine	Southampton
20.	I. Callaghan	Liverpool
21.	R. Hunt	Liverpool
22.	G. Eastham	Arsenal

Football finally came home in June 1996, when England played host to the European Championship and English football was rehabilitated in the eyes of the world.

Euro 96

With the reputation of English football on the line, it was just as important for English players and fans to behave well as it was to win the Championship. England had only just scraped into the previous European Championship in 1992, and, worse still, had failed to qualify for the 1994 World Cup. English football was definitely in the doldrums. Staging this prestigious competition was just the shot in the arm that the national game needed. Things could only get better.

At the back of everyone's mind was the secret belief that England would win again at Wembley, that it would be like the World Cup of 1966 all over again. In the event, they lost a needle match to the Germans in the semi-finals, on a penalty shootout of all things, and then the Germans went on to win the Cup. Despite this catastrophe England (now managed by Terry Venables) played better than for a long time, and everyone behaved like true sports: overall, Euro 96 was a public relations triumph for England.

The tournament kicked off at Wembley on June 8th, with a suitably impressive pageant involving St George, a smoke-belching dragon and all the other trappings of Olde Englande. England was enjoying a heatwave, which made additional demands on players used to playing in the cold or the wet. The game that followed failed to live up to the occasion: England expected to win but could only manage a draw with Switzerland. It could easily have been a defeat were it not for a great save by David Seaman. The best thing about the match was that Alan Shearer ended his two seasons' international goal drought.

England were in Group A with Scotland and Holland, as well as Switzerland. England played all their matches at Wembley, the second one being against Scotland, which England won. Highlights were a penalty save by Seaman and a spectacular goal from Gascoigne. The first half was goal-less but Scotland played better. The second half of the game was reckoned to have been the most exciting of the whole tournament. Jamie Redknapp was only on the field for half an hour but he made a great contribution to the match by starting off the manoeuvre that led to Shearer's header. Venables, feeling that his controversial choice of players had been vindicated, rated Gascoigne's goal as not only the best goal of the tournament, but the best goal of the last three major tournaments.

above: Wembley stages a spectacular opening ceremony. far left: Gascoigne celebrates his goal against Scotland. left: Sheringham tangles with Stefan Reuter at the semi-final.

When Gareth Southgate failed at the penalty shootout in the semi-final, the whole country felt bad for him. One of the first to comfort him was Stuart Pearce who had been in the same position in Italia 90: he said, "We are all in this together." Southgate, a defender, was naturally inconsolable, but was eventually able to put it into perspective by remembering the incredible atmosphere at Wembley and how proud and lucky he was "to play for my country in a tournament our generation will always remember."

According to our spies the Dutch team brought 900 pairs of shorts, 500 pairs of socks, 550 shirts, 100 tracksuits, 100 pairs of bootlaces and 140 jockstraps to Euro 96. A severe case of over-packing or were they expecting to stay for longer?

below: **Alan Shearer heads home England's goal against Germany.**

A few days later England faced Holland, needing a win to ensure a place in the final eight. Fired up by the dazzling display against Scotland, the England team played their best for years and beat the Dutch favourites 4-1. England fans were overjoyed at the return to form and very optimistic about England's chances of winning the Championship. People began to talk about destiny - always a mistake.

The quarter-finals saw England drawn against Spain. This was a match we expected to win, forgetting perhaps that Spain were unbeaten for two years. Neither side could score, which meant that the new golden goal rule had to be implemented in extra time. This was England's first experience of the sudden death situation, whereby the first team to score a goal won and the game ended there and then. Those who dreamt up the new rule cannot have realised how tense and defensive this would make the players. There were still no goals, as both sides were concentrating on not making a mistake that let the other guys take advantage. Now England faced their nightmare situation. Memories of the penalty shoot-out against Italy in the 1990 World Cup flooded back, but, luckily, everyone kept their cool. Stuart Pearce, who had missed for England in Italy, was not going to let it happen again and really put his heart in his boot for his goal. When it went in, he turned to the

crowd and roared with relief - and they roared back at him. Thanks to Seaman the saviour, England won 4-2 and went on to the semi-final to meet their nemesis.

Thirty years after the sublime World Cup victory at Wembley, England took on Germany for a place in the final. This was the real final of the Championship, whoever won this would be the favourite to beat either France or the Czech Republic. A crowd of 76,000 at Wembley and 26 million TV viewers cheered as Alan Shearer scored in the third minute. What a magnificent start. There was an equaliser soon afterwards, then the rest of the game was a roller-coaster ride of near misses and saves. Another dreaded golden goal extra time had the country on the edge of its seat, but still no goals, and then it was on to the worst case scenario - a penalty shoot out against Germany!

Five players from each team scored, but Gareth Southgate's guardian angel was off duty that night and he missed. It was up to Seaman to save the next kick from Germany - and though he was rated as the best goalkeeper in the world as a result of his performance in Euro 96, this was one he couldn't stop. Those who had wanted to see an exciting game certainly had their money's worth, but only those who paid in deutschmarks got the result they wanted. Germany's manager, Bertie

Vogts, acknowledged that his team had been lucky to win against England even though Germany had never played better.

The Final, at Wembley naturally, was a disappointment for home fans. Germany played the Czech Republic, but the outcome was predictable: Germany had already beaten the Czechs in Round One. English fans who found themselves lumbered with a ticket for the Final supported the Czechs, but the Germans won anyway - with a disputed golden goal. This was the first major event to be decided by the golden goal rule.

Even if the Final - and the result! - had been a disappointment, the 1996 European Championship had seen some brilliant football and some of the most dramatic and tense moments in the competition's history. So England didn't recreate that '66 World Cup magic, they didn't win the Cup, but they did win the UEFA Fair Play Trophy, and Alan Shearer was named as the tournament's five goal top scorer. There was no hooliganism at Wembley, and the rest of the footballing world began to consider the possibility of England hosting the World Cup in 2006. England got a result!

below: Jurgen Klinsmann the victorious German captain. right: Patrick Berger of the Czech Republic capitulates in his own way.

England's matches in the 1996 European Championship

First Round Group A

England v Switzerland 1-1
(GOALS: Shearer 23, Turkyilmaz 82 penalty)

England v Scotland 2-0
(GOALS: Shearer 52, Gascoigne 79)

England v Holland 4-1
(GOALS: Shearer 23 pen 57, Sheringham 51, 62, Kluivert 78)

	P	W	D	L	F	A	Pts
England	3	2	1	0	7	2	7
Holland	3	1	1	1	3	4	4
Scotland	3	1	1	1	1	2	4
Switzerland	3	0	1	2	1	4	1

Quarter Finals

England v Spain 0-0
(ENGLAND WON 4-2 ON PENALTIES AFTER EXTRA TIME)

Semi Finals

England v Germany 1-1
(GOALS: Shearer 3, Kuntz 16)
(GERMANY WON 6-5 ON PENALTIES AFTER EXTRA TIME)

the tartan army

Year	Score	Winner
1924	1-1	
1928	1-5	Scotland
1930	5-2	England
1932	3-0	England
1934	3-0	England
1936	1-1	
1938	0-1	Scotland
1947	1-1	
1949	1-3	Scotland
1951	2-3	Scotland
1953	2-2	
1955	7-2	England
1957	2-1	England
1959	1-0	England
1961	9-3	England
1963	1-2	Scotland
1965	2-2	
1967	2-3	Scotland
1969	4-1	England
1971	3-1	England
1973	1-0	England
1975	5-1	England
1977	1-2	Scotland
1979	3-1	England
1981	0-1	Scotland
1983	2-0	England
1986	2-1	England
1988	1-0	England
1996	2-0	England
1999	0-1	Scotland

Hadrian's Wall couldn't keep them out: every other Spring there was an invasion from over the border and their destination was Wembley Stadium.

The biennial invasion of Wembley Stadium by the Auld Enemy first took place two weeks before the stadium officially opened for the Empire Exhibition. England v Scotland had been an annual fixture since 1872 at various grounds, but Wembley soon became England's home ground.

The 1928 match excited so much interest that Scottish fans took scaling ladders with them and literally invaded the stadium to see their side teach England a never-to-be-forgotten lesson. The away win was something of a surprise as the players had been enthusiastically celebrating their victory in advance the night before. Hung over and undersized though they were, the wet weather helped them by making the pitch slick and they ran rings around the cumbersome English players. The Scottish team was thereafter referred to as the Wembley Wizards. But two years later England had its revenge and so the vendetta continued.

In 1931 the Football League stopped Scottish players from English teams playing for Scotland. In 1928, for example, team-mates from Huddersfield Town had found themselves on opposing sides, which must have been confusing. For the next couple of years the Scots would send only a thoroughly tartan team, and it seems that this fuelled nationalist pride and inevitably the contest meant more to them than it

did to the English. Fans saved for two years for the trip down south. They came in vast numbers, swathed in tartan, determined to have a fantastic day out. For 20 years Scotland did not lose at Wembley (excluding fundraising wartime matches).

According to Jimmy Greaves, who should know, the 1961 England win over Scotland was one of the greatest games ever seen at Wembley. Though Scotland played an excellent game and scored three times, they were no match for Greaves and his team-mates. In a contest known for its higher than average score, England's nine goals - three from Greaves - set a new record.

In 1967 Scotland fans were delirious with joy at beating the team that had won the World Cup a few months previously. Many Scots claimed they were the rightful World Champions. Not surprisingly this found no support whatsoever south of the border. What made the game a particularly enjoyable experience for the Scots was the attitude displayed by Jim Baxter, who could barely disguise his contempt for the World Champions.

In 1977, after a 2-1 win, the Scots had invaded the pitch and snapped one of the goalposts. Some of them dug up a piece of the hallowed Wembley turf to take home as a souvenir. It was no more than good-natured celebration, but such over-exuberance did little to

far left: **Scottish fans pull down the goal-posts after their win in 1977.**
centre left: **Loyal supporters.** left: **Gareth Southgate clears the ball from Don Hutchison in the Euro 2000 play-off.**

above: **Alex McLeish fouls Mark Hateley in 1986.**

promote Scotland's cause. With increased pressure for England to meet more overseas opposition, the fixture was looking as though its usefulness had come to an end. And with the subsequent abandonment of the British Championship, 1988 proved to be the last game for 12 years, when the Scots returned to Wembley - and another defeat - for Euro 96.

The European Championship saw the most recent return of the grudge match. The second leg of the qualifier was played at Wembley in November 1999. England had already beaten the Scots at Hampden Park a few days before and were likely to go through to the Championship. Scotland scored the only goal of the game at Wembley but it wasn't enough to scupper England's

chances. The result was that both sides were happy with the outcome: England were relieved to be going through to the next round and Scotland were satisfied that they had humiliated the English on their own doorstep. The football authorities were also pleased by the good-natured celebrating afterwards - only 27 arrests and most of them ticket touts.

European Champions

1963 European Champions Cup Final

Milan v Benfica 2-1

May 22nd

ATTENDANCE: 45,000

GOALS: Eusebio (*Benfica*) 18 mins, Altafini (*Milan*) 58 & 66 mins

REF: Holland (*England*)

PLAYERS: MILAN: Ghezzi, David, Trebbi, Benitez, C. Maldini (*capt*), Trapattoni, Pivatelli, Dino Sani, Altafini, Rivera, Mora.

BENFICA: Costa Pereira, Cavem, Cruz, Humberto, Raul, Coluna (capt), Jose Augusto, Santana, Torres, Eusebio, Simoes.

COACHES: MILAN: Rocco. BENFICA: Riera.

1968 European Champions Cup Final

Manchester United v Benfica 4-1

May 29th

ATTENDANCE: 100,000

GOALS: Charlton (*Man. U.*) 54 & 98 mins, Best (*Man. U.*) 92 mins, Kidd (*Man. U.*) 95 mins, Jaime Graca (*Benfica*) 78 mins

REF: Lo Bello (*Italy*)

PLAYERS: MANCHESTER UNITED: Stepney, Brennan, A Dunne, Crerand, Foulkes, Stiles, Best, Kidd, Charlton (*capt*), Sadler, Aston.

BENFICA: Henrique, Adolfo, Humberto, Jacinto, Cruz, Jaime Graca, Jose Augusto, Coluna (*capt*), Eusebio, Torres, Simoes.

MANAGER: MANCHESTER UNITED: Busby

COACH: BENFICA: Gloria

1971 European Champions Cup Final

Ajax Amsterdam v Panathinaikos 2-0

June 2nd

ATTENDANCE: 90,000

GOALS: Van Dijk (*Ajax*) 5 mins, Haan (*Ajax*) 87 mins

REF: Taylor (*England*)

PLAYERS: AJAX AMSTERDAM: Stuy, Suurbier, Neeskens, Vasovic (*capt*), Rijnders (*Blankenburg 46*), Hulshoff, Swart (*Haan 46*), Van Dijk, Cruyff, G Muhren, Keizer.

PANATHINAIKOS: Ekonomopoulos, Tomaras, Vlahos, Elefterakis, Kamaras, Sourpis, Gramos, Filakouris, Antoniadis, Domazos (*capt*), Kapsis.

COACHES: AJAX AMSTERDAM: Michels
PANATHINAIKOS: Puskas

1978 European Champions Cup Final

Liverpool v Club Brugge 1-0

May 10th

ATTENDANCE: 92,000

GOALS: Dalglish (*Liverpool*) 64 mins

REF: Corver (*Holland*)

PLAYERS: LIVERPOOL: Clemence, Neal, R Kennedy, E Hughes (*capt*), Thompson, Hansen, Dalglish, Case (*Heighway 63*), Fairclough, McDermott, Souness.

CLUB BRUGGE: Jensen, Bastijns (*capt*), Maes (*Volders 70*), Krieger, Leekens, Cools, De Cubber, Vandereycken, Simeon, Ku (*Sanders 60*), Sorensen.

MANAGER: LIVERPOOL: Paisley

COACH: CLUB BRUGGE: Happel

below: **Liverpool do a lap of honour after their match against Bruges.**

1992 European Champions Cup Final

Barcelona v Sampdoria 1-0

May 20th
ATTENDANCE: **70,827**
GOAL: **Koeman** (*Barcelona*) 111 mins
REF: **Schmidhuber** (*Germany*)
PLAYERS: **BARCELONA: Zubizaretta** (*capt*), **Nando, Ferrer, R Koeman, Juan Carlos, Bakero, Salinas** (*Goikoetxea 64*), **Stoichkov, M Laudrup, Guardiola** (*Alexanco 113*), **Eusebio.**
SAMPDORIA: Pagliuca, Mannini, Katanec, Pari, Vierchowod, Lanna, Lombardo, Toninho Cerezo, Vialli (*Buso 100*), **Mancini** (*capt*), **Bonetti** (*Invernizzi 72*).
COACHES: **BARCELONA: Cruyff**
SAMPDORIA: Boskov

Milan v Benfica 1963

Benfica were the defending champions and a famous team, largely because of the great Eusebio. The media were there in droves but as the fixture was held on a week day - and this was in the days when everyone had a job – the gate receipts were disappointing. The crowd wanted Benfica to win, but they didn't, thanks to a debilitating tackle on Coluna (another key player) and two goals created by Milan's Gianni Rivera for Jose Altafini.

Manchester United v Benfica 1968

The most exciting football occasion since the glorious World Cup win two years earlier was when Manchester United met Benfica to win the most prestigious European club competition. It was also a star studded event, with Eusebio and his legendary team-mates and Busby's boys including Bobby Charlton and Nobby Stiles from the England team, who had had such a great match against many of the Portuguese players in the World Cup, as well as heart throb and ace striker George Best. It was a 1-1 draw after 90 minutes, but it was in extra time that it really caught fire. Within ten minutes Manchester United had scored three goals and within half an hour they were Champions of Europe.

Ajax Amsterdam v Panathinaikos 1971

The Dutch team dominated by Johann Cruyff had no problem beating the Greeks. England fans with long memories were pleased because Panathinaikos was coached by Ferenc Puskas, whose visit to Wembley in 1953, playing for Hungary, had resulted in England's most humiliating defeat ever. They say revenge is a dish best served cold.

Liverpool v Club Brugge 1978

A year after losing in the FA Cup, Liverpool were back at Wembley to take on the team from Bruges. They slogged it out for over an hour before Dalglish, with a pass from Souness, scored the goal that won them the Cup. English club football was enjoying a good run in Europe at the time.

Barcelona v Sampdoria 1992

By now UEFA had developed a mini-league format within the competition and the next season would see this formalised into the UEFA Champions League, as it is now known. The post-Heysel ban had now been lifted and Wembley was back on the European football map. The near-capacity crowd, over half of whom had travelled from either Spain or Italy, behaved perfectly. A familiar face was back at Wembley with the Barcelona team: Johann Cruyff, who had hung up his boots, headed for the sun and become a dynamite manager. Needless to say, his team beat the cautious Italians.

european cup

The competition for national cup winners has taken place twice at Wembley Stadium, in 1965 and 1993.

1965 European Cup-Winners Cup

West Ham v 1860 Munich 2-0
19th May
ATTENDANCE: 100,000
GOALS: Sealey (*West Ham*) 70 & 72 mins
REF: Zsolt (*Hungary*)
PLAYERS: WEST HAM-Standen, Kirkup, Burkett, Peters, Brown, Moore, Sealey, Boyce, Hurst, Dear, Sissons.
TSV 1860-Radenkovic, Wagner, Kohlars, Reich, Bena, Luttrop, Heiss, Kupper Brunnenmeier, Grosser, Rebele.

1993 European Cup-Winners Cup

Parma v Antwerp 3-1
May 12th
ATTENDANCE: 37,000
GOALS: Minotti (*Parma*) 9 mins, Melli (*Parma*) 30 mins, Cuoghi (*Parma*) 83 mins, Severeyns (*Antwerp*) 11 mins
REF: Assenmacher (*Germany*)
PLAYERS: PARMA-Ballotta, Benarrivo, Di Chiara, Minotti, Apollini, Grun, Zoratto (*Pin 25*), Cuoghi, Osio (*Pizzi 65*), Melli, Brolin.
ANTWERP: Stojanovic, Brockaert, Taeymans, Smidts, Van Rethy, Segers (*Moukri 85*), Kiekens, Jakovljevic (*Van Veirdeghem 57*), Lehnoff, Severeyns, Czerniatynski.

above: **Rudy Smidts of Antwerp and Thomas Brolin of Parma jump to head the ball.** left: **Captain Bobby Moore at the civic reception for West Ham after the 1965 success.**

winners cup

above: **Nico Brockaert tackles Alberto Di Chiara in 1993.** right: **Brolin of Parma.**

West Ham v 1860 Munich 1965

A taste of things to come in the World Cup the following year, Bobby Moore, Martin Peters and Geoff Hurst showed a German team who was who. Looking back on his distinguished career, Bobby Moore said that although winning the World Cup in 1966 was the pinnacle of his career, this was the game that gave him the most satisfaction at club level. "It was the best of both worlds – playing with your mates, guys who you trained with week in and week out, and in front of your own fans in a major final on the international stage."

Parma v Antwerp 1993

A relatively new team, owned by the Parmalat Dairy company and now one of Italy's most eminent clubs, outplayed their Belgian opponents, winning 3-1. It was Wembley's second European Final in two years, the first time UEFA had awarded a venue a major competition two years running.

rugby

Wembley Stadium has been the stage of Rugby League's showpiece game, the Challenge Cup, for 72 years.

Despite still being a largely northern game, the trip down south for the big day in May is the highlight of the Rugby League calendar. One of the first sports to go professional, it was once played and watched almost exclusively in Lancashire, Yorkshire and Cumberland. During the years after the First World War, crowds at the Challenge Cup Final had steadily increased to the point where no northern ground could accommodate them. In 1928 at the 7th Annual Conference of the Rugby League a motion was passed that the final tie for each Challenge Cup should be held in London.

The choice of venue was between White City, Crystal Palace and Wembley Stadium. White City was ruled out as unsuitable early on and Crystal Palace demanded a greedy percentage of gate receipts. Arthur Elvin, at the height of his expansionist phase, saw the prestige the event would bring and offered a very reasonable deal, which the canny northerners unanimously accepted. They, too, saw the link with Wembley as prestigious: they wanted a chance to show the capital how good sports behaved on and off the field and to establish the sport on a national stage.

The shared aim between the Stadium bosses and the Rugby League was to make the first Challenge Cup Final a success, especially in terms of gate receipts. A big advertising campaign was launched and the main clubs organised coach trips to Wembley, but with half an hour to go the stadium was looking pretty empty. Honour was saved by a last minute rush to pay at the turnstiles and by 3 o'clock a very respectable crowd of 41,500 was in place. Gate receipts totalled £5,614 - almost twice the amount taken at any previous Rugby League Final.

The match itself was something of a foregone conclusion: Wigan, future undisputed stars of Wembley, took on Dewsbury who were making their first and last Wembley appearance. Wigan won 13-2.

According to legend in Yorkshire, the League Chairman paid a visit to the dressing rooms and told the players he wanted to see an open attacking game which would show the sport off to advantage. Dewsbury were known for their cautious, defensive playing and felt that this tactic would favour Wigan. They felt the game was lost before the match had started.

The Challenge Cup Final was soon established as a regular fixture. In 1932 a hiccup in scheduling occurred: the League wanted to change the date of the Cup Final to allow them to go on a tour of Australia, but Wembley was not available on the new date, so they were forced to stage the event at Central Park, Wigan's ground. Only 29,000 came to watch. This drop in the League's bank balance put paid to any who doubted Wembley's suitability once and for all.

One of the most memorable matches of the pre-war years was when royalty first graced the occasion in 1933. King George V had planned to attend but was indisposed, so Edward, Prince of Wales stood in for him. A helpful hand-out was produced for the guests which explained the crucial differences between Rugby League and Rugby Union so that they might have some idea of what was going on in the game. Whether or not they did, it was a superb match (Huddersfield 21 – 17 Warrington), with the number of points in a final a record unbroken until 1959.

above: Dale Laughton of Sheffield Eagles and Neil Cowie of Wigan Warriors, 1998. right: John Timu of London Broncos is tackled by Harris and Fleary of Leeds Rhinos, 1999. far right: Young Rhino fan.

RUGBY LEAGUE'S TOP TEAM

number of tries in a Cup Final at Wembley

Team	Total Tries
WIGAN	380
ST HELENS	205
LEEDS	170
WIDNES	135
WAKEFIELD	101
WARRINGTON	101
BRADFORD	91
FEATHERSTONE	83
HALIFAX	79
HULL	73
CASTLEFORD	56
HUDDERSFIELD	50
BARROW	44
WORKINGTON	39
HULL KR	38
HUNSLET	27
LEIGH	24
SHEFFIELD	17
LONDON	16
SALFORD	16
YORK	8
KEIGHLEY	5
DEWSBURY	2

rugby records

Highest number of tries by a player in a single cup final:
NEIL FOX scored 20 in the 1960 final.

ALEX MURPHY played and won in 4 Cup finals, was the first man to captain 3 winning sides at Wembley (St Helens, Leigh and Warrington), and was the only player-coach to win twice at Wembley.

In almost a quarter of a century there have been many memorable matches; these are the Cup Finals that stand out:

1929 WIGAN V DEWSBURY, the first final at Wembley Stadium.

1933 HUDDERSFIELD V WARRINGTON, rugby goes royal for the first time.

1938 SALFORD V BARROW, Salford were managed by the legendary Lance Todd when they won at Wembley.

1946 WAKEFIELD V WIGAN, the first match after the wartime break was notable for the last minute penalty by Billy Stott which gave Wakefield the Cup.

1946, '47,'48 BRADFORD NORTHERN'S 3 consecutive appearances at Wembley.

1954 HALIFAX V WARRINGTON, a rare draw: Warrington won the replay.

1965 WIGAN V HUNSLET, a superb, high scoring epic.

1968 LEEDS V WAKEFIELD, known as the Watersplash Final. When Don Fox missed a conversion right in front of the posts, his incredulous Leeds opponents did a victory dance in the pouring rain and the entire town of Wakefield wept (allegedly).

1988-95 Wigan's Reign of Terror.

1996 ST HELENS V BRADFORD, Robbie Paul won £100,000 as the first player to score a Wembley hat-trick.

1998 SHEFFIELD V WIGAN, underdogs, the Sheffield Eagles, beat Wembley stars Wigan.

1999 First appearance by a southern club, Richard Branson's London Broncos.

ERIC ASHTON captained Wigan six times at Wembley (1958, 1959, 1961, 1963, 1965, 1966). He later became a coach, first with Wigan, then St Helens, where he eventually became chairman of the club. He went to Wembley for the Challenge Cup Final a record 11 times, either as player, coach or chairman.

PAUL LOUGHLIN must be Rugby League's unluckiest player at Wembley. He has reached the Challenge Cup Final four times and lost each time. The first three times were with St Helens (1987,1989,1991), but in 1996 he played for Bradford Bulls who lost to - St Helens!

ROBBIE PAUL was the youngest captain of a Challenge Cup Final, at 20 years and three months when he led Bradford Bulls against St Helens, 1996.

above: **Richie Eyres of Leeds is brought down by Gary Connolly of Wigan, 1995.** right: **Franco Botica of Wigan hits the ground, 1992.**

Rugby Union has recently found a temporary home at Wembley Stadium. In 1998-9 Cardiff Arms Park was being rebuilt so Wembley became the Welsh team's home ground. It was the scene of their hammering by the All Blacks in 1997 and the French in 1998 but also the site of their victory over Scotland in 1998 and England in 1999. In 1992 Twickenham was being redeveloped so England beat Canada at Wembley Stadium.

The first televised Challenge Cup Final was in 1958, when Wigan beat Workington Town. TV coverage allowed the sport to reach a new audience and players to become stars. The Super League created by Rupert Murdoch for Sky TV in 1995 took the game another step away from its humble northern origins.

Roy Kinnear, father of the late comedy actor of the same name, played for Wigan in the very first Wembley Challenge Cup Final and scored a superb try.

The biggest attendance was 97,939 in 1969 when Castleford beat Salford 11-6. Since the all-seating policy was introduced, audiences have been near to capacity every year. The friendly invasion of northerners to Wembley is viewed by them as (in the words of Alex Murphy) "a lad's day out, the works trip, a day by the seaside and Christmas – all rolled into one."

Wembley has seen not only 64 Finals, but 7 Great Britain Internationals against Australia and New Zealand, plus two England v Australia matches in the 1995 World Cup.

Rugby Roll of Honour
League Table of Wembley Challenge Cup Finalists 1929-99

Awarding two points for winners, one for losers

team	won	lost	points
Wigan	1929, 1948, 1951, 1958, 1959, 1965, 1985, 1988, 1989, 1990, 1991, 1992, 1993, 1994, 1995	1946, 1961, 1963, 1966, 1970, 1984, 1998	37
St Helens	1956, 1961, 1966, 1972, 1976, 1996, 1997	1930, 1953, 1978, 1987, 1989, 1991	20
Widnes	1930, 1937, 1964, 1975, 1979, 1981, 1984	1934, 1950, 1976 1977, 1982, 1993	20
Leeds	1936, 1957, 1968, 1977, 1978, 1999	1947, 1971, 1972, 1994, 1995	17
Halifax	1931, 1939, 1987	1949, 1954, 1956, 1988	10
Wakefield	1946, 1960, 1962, 1963	1968, 1979	10
Warrington	1950, 1954, 1974	1933, 1936, 1975, 1990	10
Castleford	1935, 1969, 1970, 1986	1992	9
Bradford	1947, 1949	1948, 1973, 1996, 1997	8
Featherstone	1967, 1973, 1983	1952, 1974	8
Hull	1982	1959, 1960, 1980, 1983, 1985	7
Barrow	1955	1938, 1951, 1957, 1967	6
Huddersfield	1933, 1953	1935, 1962	6
Hull KR	1980	1964, 1981, 1988	5
Salford	1938	1939, 1969	4
Workington	1952	1955, 1958	4
Hunslet	1934	1965	3
Leigh	1971		2
Sheffield	1998		2
Dewsbury		1929	1
Keighley		1937	1
London		1999	1
York		1931	1

WONDERFUL

When it comes to Wembley wins,

above: **Andy Gregory acknowledges the crowd after beating Castleford, 1992.**

Shaun Edwards At 17

Edwards was the youngest player ever in a Cup Final (1984 Widnes v Wigan). His maturity coincided, though it was no coincidence, with Wigan's Glory Days. He played in eight consecutive cup ties and won all of them, an unbroken record in the sport. His finest hour was when he played on with a broken cheekbone and eye socket, despite being in agony and barely able to see, after a shoulder charge in the 1990 final against Warrington. It takes a tough guy to play a tough game!

Although they won the first ever Challenge Cup Final at Wembley in 1929, there was nothing to suggest that the team from Wigan would one day dominate Rugby League. They had to wait until after the war before they came to Wembley again. They lost in 1946 to Wakefield, but they kept at it and returned to triumph over Bradford in 1948.

Over the next 20 years or so they had their moments - 1951,'58,'59,'65 – and a few near misses – 1961,'63,'66, '70 - like any other club, but it wasn't until the 1980s that they really came on stream. Another near miss in 1984, followed by a win in 1985, a two year blip then WHAM – eight solid years of Wembley wins. The Stadium became the club's second home and the silver Silk Cut Challenge Cup became part of the furniture at Wigan's clubhouse.

Like a snowball gathering snow and speed as it rolls downhill, Wigan's success led to more success: the Wembley gate receipts plus all the associated income from the wins made the club rich enough to buy the best. They were soon in a different financial league from the rest of the clubs and it began to be an unfair contest. However, the gravy train stopped in February 1996 with a shuddering halt when a shock defeat by Salford put them out of the Cup. That year the Final was between their arch rivals St Helens (who won) and Bradford: it was open season and the Cup was up for grabs once more.

Back at Wigan there was a financial crisis at the club: top players' wages and massive transfer fees relied on the high income that derived from winning the Cup. Now the books didn't balance. The directors faced legal proceedings. No wonder the players were off their game for a few seasons. Meanwhile the sport in general had been shaken up and given a huge cash injection by the Super League deal with Sky TV in

1995. Other clubs could now afford top players and coaches. When Wigan got their act together and made it through to the finals again in 1998, they were defeated by a relatively recent club, the Sheffield Eagles.

Why did the Wigan phenomenon happen? Part of the reason must come down to the right collection of people being together at the right time. Maurice Lindsay, since described as one of the most influential men in the sport, got a seat on the board at Wigan at about the same time as they took on Alex Murphy as coach and recruited teen star Shaun Edwards. The talent pool later included Martin Offiah, Ellery Hanley, Graeme West, Brett Kenny and Andy Gregory. TV coverage of the sport generated interest in the club and its charismatic players beyond the traditional heartland of the sport. The Wigan success story gave the game glamour and the media an angle - it is probably what made Rupert Murdoch get out his chequebook.

below: **Shawn Edwards after the 1988 victory over Halifax.**

WIGAN

Wigan are the champions.

above: The 1988 Wigan team celebrate another triumph. top right: Sam Panapa after the win over Widnes, 1993.

Alex Murphy Though associated nowadays with Wigan's Golden Era, Murphy wasn't always a Wigan man. Back in 1966 he played for St Helens against Wigan in the Cup Final. His side won and he couldn't resist rubbing the other side's noses in it; he sent them a telegram saying "Roses are red, violets are blue. St Helens 21, Wigan 2."

Probably the proudest moment of his distinguished career took place at Wembley. Fifteen minutes before the final whistle in the 1971 Leigh v Leeds Final, Murphy was knocked to the ground by Syd Hughes (who became the first rugby player to be sent off in a Cup Final). Murphy was carried off on a stretcher, but returned a few minutes later, still groggy according to eye witnesses, to finish the game and be named Man of the Match. The unthinkable had happened, little Leigh (Murphy's club making their one and only Wembley appearance) had beaten the favourites, who, according to Murphy, thought all they had to do was turn up for the match. Leeds supporters claimed that Murphy took a dive to get someone sent off, but he didn't need to as Leigh were already ahead. Nevertheless, it suited his mischievous nature to wait 20 years before denying it.

Whatever club he played for, Wembley remains a special place for him and he claims getting your first winner's medal at Wembley is better than winning the lottery.

the olympic games

When Wembley Stadium hosted the Olympic Games in 1948, sport was able to help heal the wounds of a devastating world war.

The years after the Second World War were tough in Britain. Food was rationed at least as much as during the war and the country was in dire straits economically. Millions of people were trying to adjust to being back on civvy street, coping with the loss of loved ones, homes and the life they knew before. The last thing the country needed was to splash out on a frivolous expense like staging the XIV Olympiad.

Not so, said Arthur Elvin, now Sir Arthur for services to sport. What the country needs - what the world needs - is a celebration of peace and unity. Before the war Britain had been pegged for the 1944 Olympics, which of course never happened. The Americans had offered to stage the first post-war games, because only they could bear the cost, but it was soon realised that few European countries could afford to send a squad across the Atlantic. If the

games were to take place they should be in Europe and Elvin was able to persuade the authorities that Britain was the only possible place.

Naturally Wembley formed the basis for the bid and in less than two years extensive modernisation took place within the stadium (new dressing rooms, terraces, car parks, running track and scoreboard) and in the immediate area. Wembley Park tube station was enlarged to cope with the extra crowds and a new road, Olympic Way, was built to direct visitors straight from the station to the stadium. Contestants made their own way to the stadium on the tube from their less than glamorous digs elsewhere in London.

All was ready on time and the Opening Ceremony was held at Wembley Stadium on July 29th in the presence of King George VI, Queen Elizabeth, Queen Mary, Princess

The original athletics track had been laid at Wembley for the 1924 Empire Exhibition but it was now buried under the greyhound track. 100 men were required to recreate a track fit for world class athletes. They laid a top dressing of 800 tons of cinders from the fireplaces of Leicester, but no one remembers what was so special about Leicester cinders.

On the day of the Marathon, a man claiming to be Dorando Pietri, who had collapsed just before the White City finish line in the 1908 London Games, was feted in the Royal Box. He turned out to be an imposter, an Italian from Birmingham.

above: **Fanny Blankers-Koen of Holland on her way to winning the women's 80m hurdles.** right: **The Olympic torch arrives at Wembley.**

Margaret and other members of the royal family. Princess Elizabeth, as our present Queen then was, was pregnant at the time and had to stay at home. The Olympic Torch was carried into the stadium by John Mark, a 22-year-old Cambridge University quarter-miler. There was a 21-gun salute and 7,000 pigeons (symbolising doves of peace and donated by pigeon-fanciers all over the country following a public appeal) were released. A crowd of 82,000 watched as the British team captain, Donald Finlay, took the Olympic Oath, promising to participate "in the true spirit of sportsmanship, for the honour of our country and for the glory of sport."

59 countries took part in the Olympics - notable exceptions being Germany and the USSR. Wembley Stadium staged 33 track and field events and was the scene of 17 new world and Olympic records, including two by Emil Zatopek (5000m and 10,000m). The star of the Wembley events was Fanny Blankers-Koen, a 30-year-old Dutch housewife and mother

of two. She won four gold medals and set a new world and Olympic record in the 80m hurdles, beating Britain's great hope, Maureen Gardner, in a photo-finish. She delighted the public with her jolly wholesomeness and her claim that she drank three litres (almost six pints) of milk a day must have thrilled farmers and milkmen.

The subject of the contestants' diet was contentious. Those who were opposed to the idea of hosting the games were particularly focussed on how unfair it was to have well-fed Americans competing against under-nourished Europeans. Everybody knew that Americans ate steak three times a day, whereas the British were living on powdered egg and Spam! In fact the results seem to bear this out: the USA won more gold medals than any other country in the Games.

Britain's golds were not won at Wembley - they were for rowing and yachting - but the warmth and the sportsmanship of the Wembley crowd was remarked upon and applauded by all those who took part.

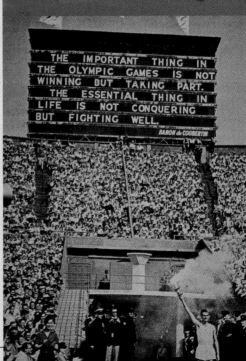

THE IMPORTANT THING IN THE OLYMPIC GAMES IS NOT WINNING BUT TAKING PART. THE ESSENTIAL THING IN LIFE IS NOT CONQUERING BUT FIGHTING WELL.

BARON de COUBERTIN

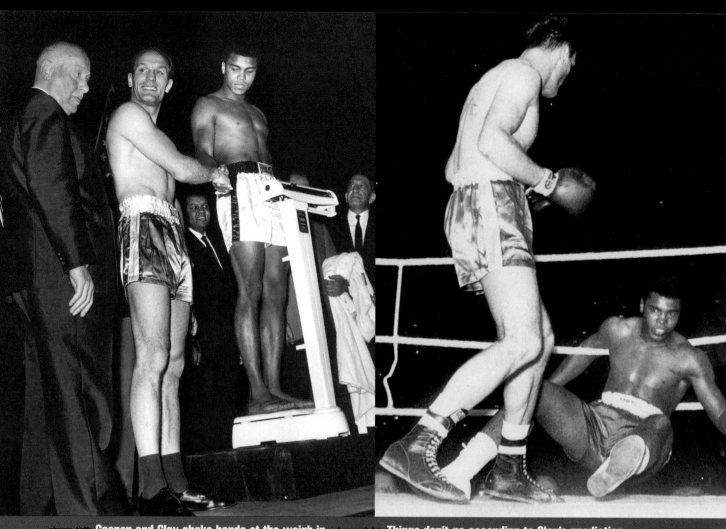

above left: **Cooper and Clay shake hands at the weigh-in.** above right: **Things don't go according to Clay's prediction.**
below: **Cooper on the attack.** far right: **Promotor Don King with Frank Bruno.**

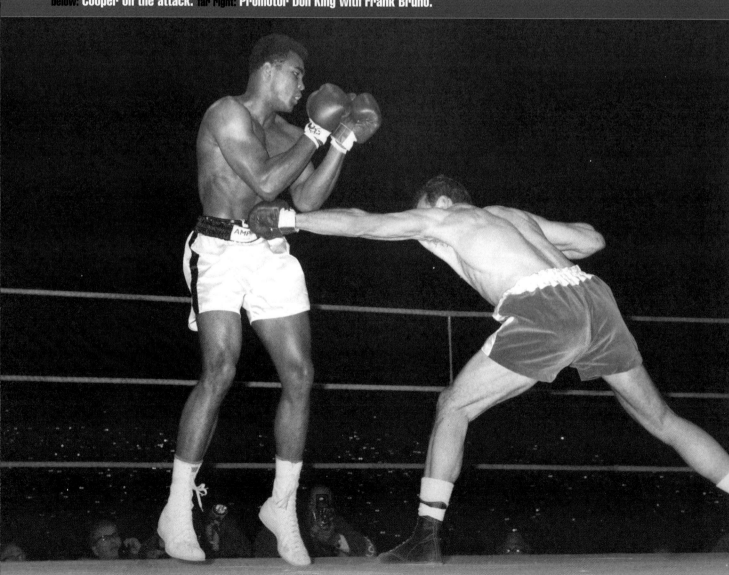

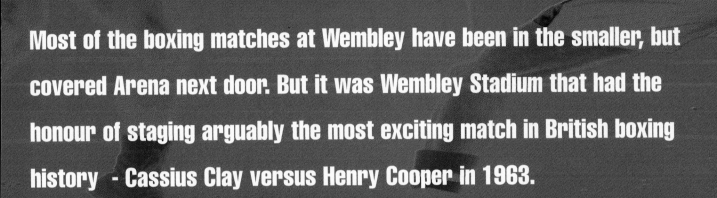

Most of the boxing matches at Wembley have been in the smaller, but covered Arena next door. But it was Wembley Stadium that had the honour of staging arguably the most exciting match in British boxing history - Cassius Clay versus Henry Cooper in 1963.

Boxing

Cassius Clay, not yet known as Muhammed Ali, was a media dream; a very young, very articulate and very handsome black American, something of a novelty in Britain then. In the days before the fight he delighted the public with his cheeky and boastful rhyming couplets: "If he give me jive, he fall in five." You couldn't dislike him, plus, he was a brilliant fighter. His opponent was the much older Henry Cooper, the best liked man in British boxing. Whoever won the public would be happy.

Clay was confident of winning and strode into the ring wearing a cardboard crown, promising to "whup" Cooper "like I'm his daddy". Cooper was unfazed and proceeded to win the first two rounds. Unfortunately Cooper had a tendency to cut easily and in round three his left eyebrow was cut and began to bleed heavily. Despite his injury Cooper landed the most famous punch thrown in a British ring on Clay in round four. " 'Enery's 'ammer", his powerful left hook, hit Clay's jaw and knocked him down. Clay was literally saved by the bell. Had that punch come a few seconds earlier, he would have been counted out and the course of

boxing history might have been changed, but as it was Clay used the one-minute interval to recover and then curiously his glove seemed to have become untied, which took another minute to fix. By the time he came out again he was back on form and devoted his attention to Cooper's cut so effectively that the fight was stopped in round five as predicted.

Clay's next fight saw him beat Sonny Liston to become Heavyweight Champion of the World. Cooper was satisfied with his performance and has been dining out on his reminiscences of that night ever since.

There'll probably never be another night like it, but September 2nd 1995 was a night for celebrating when another popular British boxer, Frank Bruno, braved the open air of Wembley Stadium to become champion of the world. He beat Oliver McCall on points for the WBC World Title. Bruno is the only fighter to top the bill at Wembley Stadium twice. Wembley Arena just wasn't big enough for the man! He said "Whatever happens to me now, if I'm shot tomorrow, if I fall under a bus, if I'm run over by a train, nobody can ever take this away from me. No wonder I love Wembley!"

other sports at Wembley

When Arthur Elvin took hold of the reins at Wembley the stadium had to be run as a business. Great occasions like Cup Finals and prestigious internationals were all very well, but they didn't provide the regular income needed to keep the stadium up to scratch. Less glamorous sports events like greyhound racing and speedway are what really paid the rent.

above: Wembley's bread and butter fixtures were greyhound racing and speedway before the war. Women's hockey and American football were some of Wembley's other sports.

Baseball has been played at Wembley Stadium on two occasions. In 1934 the US Ambassador organised a match between two teams from the USS *New Orleans* "with one or two London players assisting," according to the programme. In 1943 the US Air Force played the US Ground Force in front of a largely American crowd

Greyhound Racing Greyhound racing was a popular spectator sport in the USA in the 1920s. A mechanical hare which could be used on an oval circuit had been invented and the idea was brought to Britain by Charles A Munn, who formed the Greyhound Racing Association with three others. The sport took off and within two years there were 17 GRA courses in Britain. Elvin the entrepreneur was quick to see the potential and spent £90,000 - a fortune in those days - on a new track, lighting and kennels etc. The idea was that Wembley Stadium would be the Ascot of greyhound racing.

The first night, December 10th 1927, was attended by 50,000 and from then on Wembley Stadium became one of the premier tracks in the country. In the first year over one and a half million people came to Wembley to watch the dogs. The first trophy event in the sport, the Padgett Cup, was staged there. This event was only for dogs bred in Wembley's own kennels, which soon developed an excellent reputation and bred many winners. In the years up to the Second World War greyhound racing was Britain's biggest spectator sport: it may have had a cloth cap image but in reality there were many titled owners and enthusiasts like the Marquis of Bath.

George Stanton, a former general manager of Wembley Stadium, said: "For the best part of 50 years the greyhounds have been the stadium's bread and butter. Soccer and the like were the jam, but without the dogs I doubt we would have survived." However though the greyhounds raced until 1998, interest had declined since the Fifties due to television and the availability of other leisure pursuits.

Speedway Speedway was another new sport brought to Britain from abroad in the 1920s. It was introduced to this country by showman Johnnie Hoskins who had found racing motorbikes on dirt tracks to be very popular at Australian country shows. Once greyhound racing was established at Wembley Arthur Elvin turned his attention to speedway which had drawn a record crowd of 78,000 at White City. Hoskins was hired to build a winning side, the Wembley Lions, and on May 16th 1929 speedway was launched at Wembley. Takings were disappointing at first, despite an exten-

sive advertising campaign, and it wasn't until Elvin came up with the idea of forming a supporters' club that the sport took off at Wembley.

At the end of the first season the Wembley Speedway Supporters' Club, who enjoyed reduced admission plus various fringe benefits, had almost 20,000 members. By 1948 it had a 61,000 membership, the biggest in the world. Wembley became the annual venue for the World Final in 1936 and the Wembley Lions won the League Championship 10 times in 18 seasons. In 1946 1,211,355 tickets were sold for 22 fixtures, a weekly average over the season of over 55,000. Once again Wembley Stadium had become the premier venue of a successful sport.

Speedway meetings were more than just races at Wembley. There were stunt shows and circus acts between races, and track staff marched around to the tune of *The March of the Gladiators*. Arthur Elvin took a close interest in the fortunes of the home team and would reportedly be on the phone to the manager if they lost demanding to know the

reason why.

Following Elvin's sudden death in 1957 it took his fellow directors only two weeks to decide to close down the club. There was an attempt to reintroduce League racing in 1970-71 and the World Final continued to be staged on a three-year cycle at Wembley Stadium. Finally pressure from The Football Association, who complained about having to lift and relay the corners of the pitch to accommodate the shale track, saw the chequered flag finally lowered at Wembley in 1981.

American Football Wembley Stadium played a major part in the on-going attempt to interest the British public in American Football. By the 1980s it was obvious that if American Football were to take off in Britain there was only one place where it would happen - Wembley Stadium - finally famous in America after Live Aid.

Pete Rozell, commissioner of American Football's National Football League, and Tex Schramm, president of Dallas Cowboys organised the first

American Bowl on August 3rd 1986, as part of their mission to spread the word worldwide. Amidst a carnival atmosphere, 82,000 watched the Chicago Bears beat the Dallas Cowboys 17-6 in the pouring rain.

The glamour of gridiron, the cheerleaders with their pompoms and implants, the much hyped reputation of giants like The Fridge (aka William Perry), all went down well in Britain and the NFL returned the American Bowl game to Wembley stadium for a further seven years.

In 1991 a World League of American Football was set up and Wembley was one of ten teams in it. Barcelona, Frankfurt, Montreal and six US cities were the others. Calling themselves the London Monarchs, the Wembley team won their first nine games and then triumphed in the World Bowl Final against Barcelona Dragons. A crowd of 61,000 waved Union Jacks and sang *We Will Rock You*. In 1992, however, interest in the sport had diminished and the use of a stadium for its games was no longer justified.

One of the **strangest sporting events** at Wembley was the construction of a 154 ft (47m) ski jumping ramp covered with **artificial snow**. In 1961 40 visiting competitors, including several Olympic medallists, came to Wembley for a two-day ski jumping competition. It took 36 hours to erect the giant ramp and **a lot of ice crushing** machines to keep the snow from melting as the event took place in June!

Music at Wembley

There was always music at Wembley - massed bands and community singing were a traditional warm-up to Cup Finals for years – but the event that defined Wembley Stadium as the premier rock venue was Live Aid.

On Saturday July 13th 1985 the 12 hour concert was watched by 74,000 in the stadium and 1.4 billion television viewers all over the world, each one with a massive lump in the throat. This was no ordinary super-gig, this was the rock community's finest hour, a chance to show that there is more to rock than sex and drugs. Inspired by a news report on BBC television of mass starvation on an almost biblical scale in Ethiopia, Bob Geldof, the singer of The Boomtown Rats, a once successful but fading band, had already raised millions of pounds for famine relief with the Band Aid single *Do They Know It's Christmas*? Using the same overwhelming drive and commitment, not to mention nagging, blagging and bullying, Geldof managed to get all the important acts of the day to reorganise their schedules and agree to appear for free for Live Aid.

When it came to choosing a venue, Hyde Park was briefly considered, but there really was nowhere more suitable than Wembley Stadium. Wembley gave the event authority, the TV companies involved were happy with the facilities there and, most important of all, the stadium's historic association with decades of drama and positive emotion meant that it just felt right. The staging of the concert was organised in three short weeks and was complicated by the fact that there was a satellite link with JFK Stadium in Philadelphia where the American arm of the event was being staged. From 5pm (London time) alternate sets were broadcast.

At 12 noon Status Quo kicked off at Wembley with *Rocking All Over The World*. Acts like David Bowie, Elton John, U2, The Who, Dire Straits and Queen (generally reckoned to have given the best performance that day) were interspersed with reports from Ethiopia and appeals for donations. Everyone forgave Bob Geldof, looking like he hadn't slept for a week, for saying a rude word on live telly while exhorting the public to empty their pockets. If there were any foul-ups (and there must have been) the only one the public was aware of was when Paul McCartney's microphone went dead for the *Let It Be* finale.

£10 million was raised that day alone. An uplifting and life-changing event for many, and one that established Wembley's reputation in music, but it was not the first rock concert to be held in the stadium. That historic honour went to the London Rock'n'Roll Show, billed as a Music Festival, showcasing the talents of Fifties legends like Little Richard, Jerry Lee Lewis, Chuck Berry, Bill Haley and Bo Diddley. Like Live Aid it was an all day, 12 hour event. For those that like to know these kind of things: the first ever band on stage was The Houseshakers and the first ever solo performer was Billy Fury.

The first single act to do a gig at Wembley Stadium was American supergroup Crosby, Stills, Nash and Young in 1974. This signalled a change in rock

performance that saw the end of American megastars touring the provinces; a single appearance - one night's work - could sell as many tickets as a tour. However, a show at Wembley was always a special occasion whichever side of the footlights you were on. To sell out at Wembley Stadium is the ultimate career achievement for a rock star. To go to a gig at Wembley Stadium is looked forward to and saved up for months in advance - just like a Cup Final.

Artists who have performed at Wembley include most of the great names of pop history: The Beach Boys, The Who, Simon & Garfunkel, The Rolling Stones, Elton John, Bob Dylan, Bruce Springsteen, David Bowie, Prince, Jean-Michel Jarre, Guns N Roses, Eric Clapton, Simply Red, Genesis, Pink Floyd, U2, The Eagles, Madonna, Michael Jackson, Tina Turner, Bryan Adams, Rod Stewart, Wham, The Three Tenors and The Spice Girls. Many more have appeared in multi-artist fund-raising or tribute concerts like Amnesty International, Nelson Mandela's 70th Birthday Party, the Freddie Mercury memorial concert and Net Aid. Records were broken at these events: Michael Jackson has been seen by well over a million people in his Wembley Stadium appearances; 83,000 squeezed in to see Rod Stewart, a one-event attendance record.

You don't have to be a football fan for Wembley Stadium to have a special place in your heart. Local residents will have a couple of peaceful years but no doubt the new stadium will soon be rocking to an even bigger and better beat in 2003!

the final whistle

Now Wembley Stadium, the Grand Old
Lady of British sport and spectacular, is
set to close her doors for the last time.
The events that took place within those
walls will remain in the memories of
those who witnessed or participated in
them long after the building is demolished. Now we look forward to the new
Wembley National Stadium, a world-
class venue fit for 21st century heroes
and an architectural landmark to boot.
The spirits of sports stars long dead can
remain at peace for the Twin Towers
may tumble, but the Legend never dies:
Long Live Wembley Stadium.